All-Terrain Bicycling

All-Terrain Bicycling

Charles Coombs

HENRY HOLT AND COMPANY / NEW YORK

Library of Congress Cataloging-in-Publication Data
Coombs, Charles Ira, 1914–
All-terrain bicycling.
Includes index.
1. All terrain cycling. 2. All terrain bicycles.
I. Title
GV1043.7.C66 1987   796.6   86-14980
ISBN 0-8050-0204-9

Henry Holt books are available at special discounts
for bulk purchases for sales promotions, premiums,
fund-raising, or educational use. Special editions
or book excerpts can also be created to specification.

For details, contact:

Special Sales Director
Henry Holt & Co., Inc.
115 West 18th Street
New York, New York 10011

Designer: Victoria Hartman
Printed in the United States of America
4   5   6   7   8   9   10

With the exception of those individually credited,
all photographs are by the author.

To Lee,
son and sometimes partner
in the photo lab . . . but first,
and always, son.

Contents

Acknowledgments

There has never been another time in history when so many people are having so much fun and so many adventures on bicycles. Bikes are everywhere, being ridden by virtually everyone, regardless of size, sex, or age.

It seemed that I had just finished writing a book on the wild and woolly two-wheeled sport of bicycle motocross (BMX) when I became aware of a new type of bicycle constructed for a new style of riding—popularly referred to as mountain biking—but also known as all-terrain or off-road bicycling. It seemed that bicycles were venturing into areas where bicycles were never meant to go.

A little snooping around Ron Jacobson's Westlake Cyclery, my favorite bike shop, and shooting the breeze with a few enthusiasts of the fat-tire machines convinced me that this, indeed, was a promising new area of two-wheelers to explore.

In no time at all I hung my ten-speed on the garage rafters, at least temporarily, got hold of an eighteen-speed all-terrain bike and began rubbing elbows with eager young pedalers who were glorying in the exciting field of all-terrain bicycling. Their enthusiasm added an essential spark to my research, which I tried to capture with both pencil and camera.

I would particularly like to thank Neill Humphrey and Peter Sullivan, extraordinary cyclists, who showed me how it was done and cavorted before my camera for the color jacket and assorted photos within the book.

Glenn Odell, head of the National Off-Road Bicycle Association (NORBA), was kind enough to check out my manuscript and make some helpful suggestions.

Then, too, assorted manufacturers, suppliers of biking paraphernalia, and promoters of all-terrain biking were quick to lend a hand to my efforts. To name a few, I'm indebted to Redline Engineering, Gant Corporation, Fisher Mountain Bikes, Cannondale, Schwinn, Moots, Bike Nashbar, Cycles Peugeot, and Bell Helmets for their help with data and pictures. Charles Kelly, editor of *Fat-Tire Flyer*, and David Moser of the International Bicycle Fund gave support beyond any call of duty.

To all of these people, plus any others who may have slipped my sometimes flagging memory, many thanks.

—Charles ("Chick") Coombs
Westlake Village, California
1987

1

All-Terrain Biking

Y ou climb a steep mountain trail, slog along a mossy streambed, or plunge down a rutted logging road. In winter you may even follow some snowmobile tracks across a cotton-colored meadow, or slither gingerly over a frozen lake. And, to add zest to the action, you do it all on a bicycle. Not a typical everyday bicycle, but a balloon-tired, ruggedly constructed, lightweight machine called a *mountain bike,* an *off-road bike,* a *fat-tire bike,* or an *all-terrain bike (ATB).*

Basically, your all-terrain bike differs from most other bikes in that it is designed and built to provide a stable ride and withstand the beating it gets while jumping and jolting over rough, punishing terrain. That is what off-road biking is largely about.

Off-road bicycling in its most adventuresome form tests both machine and rider far beyond the demands of normal biking. It takes you off the beaten track, away from traffic snarls, noxious odors, the roar of the city, and other urban aggravations and hazards. In essence, off-road bicycling transports you beyond where the pavement ends. It takes you closer to nature, where trees, streams, and quiet mountains beckon.

Off-road bicycling is not a brand-new invention, although the machines, the locales, and the riding techniques have changed. The changes came about because modern-day riders wanted to go

All-terrain biking takes you off the beaten track. *Los Angeles YMCA*

places and do things that had long been out of the reach of traditional cyclists.

The roots of off-road biking can be traced to the very beginnings of bicycle history. Around 1869 the first pedal-powered *velocipede* arrived in America from Europe. It had wooden wheels, solid steel rims with no tires, and a rigid frame. Called a "boneshaker," it was propelled like a kid's tricycle. The pedals were attached directly to the front wheel, and it took one full rotation of the pedals to produce a single turn of the front wheel. This made progress slow and strenuous. There were no chains, wheel bearings, or gearing of any kind. In order to slow down or stop, the rider simply dragged his or her feet.

Then someone realized that since one pedal rotation turned the front wheel once, a bigger wheel would cover more distance with each pedal stroke. The result was a very high-wheeled bike, called the "ordinary," which began to appear on America's streets in the mid-1870s. An odd-looking contraption on which the rider was seated precariously high and directly over the 5-foot-diameter front wheel, the ordinary was a difficult machine to mount, and quite top-heavy and unstable. Bruising and bone-breaking spills were common. But for about a decade the big-wheeled ordinaries were common sights on the dirt and cobblestoned streets of America.

By 1890 chain-driven bikes began to appear. They had smaller wheels, and the pedals were mounted low on a triangular frame instead of on the front wheel. The gearing consisted of a chain that looped over the teeth of a large front sprocket and a small rear one. Thus, each rotation of the pedals produced extra speed and distance. Low and relatively secure, the new bicycle was appropriately called a "safety."

Around the same time, air-inflated tires were developed. Their soft, cushioning effect took much of the bone-jarring roughness out of a ride. Owned and ridden largely by adults, these relatively high-priced machines became popular and largely replaced the horse and

The high-wheeled "ordinary" was the rage of the late nineteenth century. *Bicycle Institute of America*

buggy as a means of simple transportation in America around the turn of the century.

With the safety bike, the first big bicycle boom got under way and spread to many parts of the world. Hundreds of manufacturers, large and small, were soon turning out about 2 million bicycles a year in America alone. The bicycles manufactured then were quite similar to some of today's simple, single-speed vehicles.

But the biking boom tapered off as automobiles began to be mass-produced. Adults now turned their interests from foot-powered bicycles to gasoline-powered automobiles. Bicycling was turned over to the children, who eagerly took to it. Soon most of the boys and girls in the country were bicycling to school, to a friend's house, or happily over hill and dale.

Around the turn of the century, "safety" bicycles largely replaced the horse and buggy. *The Bettmann Archive*

Early in this century bicycling became a family activity, and remains so. *Bicycle Institute of America*

When World War II broke out, suddenly all available metal was needed for tanks, planes, and weapons. Bicycle manufacturers switched their material, tools, and production skills toward helping the war effort.

It was during this worldwide conflict that American servicemen stationed in Europe became familiar with a lightweight, thin-tired bicycle called the *English racer*. They became acquainted with revolutionary gearshift bikes that had three-speed *hubs*. These bikes could be shifted into low or high gears, which was of great benefit for climbing hills or speeding along a straightaway. The machines were a welcome change from the heavy, single-speed, balloon-tired *clunkers* that Americans were accustomed to riding.

After the war, some of the GI's brought the new lightweight bikes home with them. Even as they were showing off their bikes, newer models were being developed in Europe. More efficient hand brakes were replacing the less reliable and more complicated coaster brakes. Stronger wheels were used on light frames.

In the 1960s a multi-sprocket speed-changing system operated by a *derailleur* (dee-ráil-yurr), a French word meaning gearshift, was invented. Cyclists then had five, ten, or even fifteen different speeds from which to choose. The intricate device derails, or shifts, the bike *chain* from one set of front and rear *sprockets* to another. By simply down-shifting to a low gear, the rider could slowly climb almost any hill without undue effort. Shifting to a high gear, he could pedal over level ground at wind-whistling speed.

Presto! With the lightweight multi-gear machines a new bike boom was soon under way. It extended through the 1960s and 1970s. The heavy, balloon-tired, single-speed "newsboy" bicycles that had served generations of young people both at work and play gave way to the new, fast, skinny-tired flyers.

But these sensitive whippetlike lightweights had definite draw-backs. They were fine for racing or touring, as long as they were kept on smooth, hard-surfaced roads, avoiding ditches, street

Following World War II, European lightweight racing bikes were eagerly adopted by Americans. *Schwinn Bicycle Company*

gratings, ruts, curbs, loose dirt, and other hazards to their skinny tires. Fine bikes though they were—and are—the lightweights simply were not suited to rough riding.

Yet some young people had their own ideas about what they wanted to do with their bikes. Always restless, they longed to jump curbs, soar over stumps, lay their bikes down in knee-scraping skids, and generally push their bikes to the edge of destruction. Often they pushed too far, and many bikes broke down, or were "trashed," as it came to be called.

The riders needed something more durable to withstand their recklessness. Bicycle manufacturers sensed their needs and produced an array of low-slung, small-wheeled, stripped-down dirt bikes that they labeled BMX, initials that stand for bicycle motocross. The BMXers and their tough little machines began emulating their older brothers, who did their hill climbing and dirt riding on gasoline-powered vehicles in what they called motorcycle motocross, or MX.

From the 1970s on, the BMXers and their sturdy machines with the 20-inch wheels, the high-rise handlebars, and the knobby tires have been very much in evidence on streets, around schools, and in stiff competition on dirt obstacle courses scattered around the country.

In time, BMXers began to venture into the backcountry, well off the beaten track, with their versatile little bikes. To some extent they set the style for off-road bicycling as it is known today.

BMX machines are normally single-speed bicycles and are not well adapted to extended hill climbing or riding through soft dirt or mud. Still, many carefree, risk-prone cyclists had the youthful determination to explore further into areas where bicycles were never designed to go. So, in order to explore rough-terrain riding, they needed a new, sturdier, specialized vehicle.

In northern California a group of fun-loving young men and women began handcrafting and riding bikes that they could maneuver over rutted backcountry trails without having them break down or leave parts scattered in their wake. They scrounged around and dug up some old heavy-duty frames and a few rusty spoked wheels

There are similarities between BMX and all-terrain bike riding. *Jim Veltman* (left), *Gant Corporation* (right)

that had once been used on old classic clunker bikes such as the Schwinn Excelsior or the ancient J. C. Higgins—ruggedly built newsboy bikes formerly sold through Sears, Roebuck stores. They poked around the back rooms of bicycle shops and searched dark corners of garages for dusty two-wheeled relics from which they could cannibalize parts. They looked for the biggest, knobbiest tires they could find that would hold to the loose dirt without sinking up to the wheel hubs. They assembled some odd-looking bikes from assorted salvaged parts. They put ten-speed derailleurs on some. Others stuck to simple coaster-brake hubs having a single gear, or three at most.

Picking a steep hill that had the mere semblance of a trail zigzagging down its side, these young pioneers of off-road bicycling shoved off down the slope. Plunging downward, they tumbled on gravel corners, crashed into unyielding boulders, and scratched themselves mercilessly on tree trunks and spiny bushes. The few who reached the bottom relatively unscathed glanced down at their smoking coaster brakes and were excited at having pushed their new breed of bicycle to the edge of destruction.

However, before the rider could again challenge the hill, he had to let the smoking brakes cool off, then repack them with grease. Thus the hill was dubbed "Repack." It was there on Repack Hill, across the bay from San Francisco, that what came to be known as all-terrain biking got its start. At least, that is how popular history has it. There are some who claim that they were all-terrain biking long before then . . . and who's to argue?

Meanwhile, at roughly the same time, another segment of cyclists began adapting to a moderately heavy, large-tired machine called a "beach cruiser." The cruisers are quite simple, having few of the frailties to which skinny-tired ten-speeders so often fall prey. Some cruisers are single-speed; others have multiple sprockets and an extra number of gears for mild forms of off-road riding. Cruisers are durable and versatile enough to meet the needs of a large number of cyclists, whether they are students, commuters, or weekend recreationists. Cruisers and all-terrain bikes are not so very far apart when you compare their ability to maneuver in sand and dirt. But cruisers are somewhat heavier machines, and are not well-suited to the really rough off-road usage that the all-out, competitive all-terrain bikes undergo.

Certainly one cannot ignore the host of ten-speed enthusiasts who still stand staunchly by their skinny-tired lightweight road and touring bikes. In fact, their numbers continue to increase. The ten-speeds still remain the backbone of the bicycling industry.

But there remains a growing population of what have come to be

Cyclists enjoy all-out action on their all-terrain bikes. *Fisher Mountain Bikes*

called *gonzo* cyclists. True adventurers with a penchant for derring-do, they are determined to ride their bikes over terrain where once only mules or jeeps could go. For a while, they handmade their machines. As converts to the sport multiplied, the "garage factories" were unable to keep up with the demand for all-terrain bikes.

By the mid-1980s, all major bicycle manufacturers were becoming aware of the trend toward off-road biking. They adopted the basic designs and began producing thousands of rugged, fat-tired bikes. Due to specialization and handcrafting, early off-road bikes were quite expensive. With mass production they soon became no more costly than a decent ten-speed, a beach cruiser, or a well-constructed BMX bicycle.

Indeed, all-terrain bikes, regardless of brand, were soon circling the globe. Today all-terrain bikes can be seen crossing the shim-

A group of pioneering off-road bikers raft across an African river.
International Bicycle Fund/David Moser

All-terrain bikers enjoy exciting adventures in exotic lands. *International Bicycle Fund/David Moser*

mering sands of Death Valley. They have plied the African veldt and climbed Mount Kilimanjaro. They have reached the ancient Incan ruins of Machu Picchu in Peru and have crossed the vast steppes of Mongolia. They are seen as regularly in Japan as on the dirt roads of

New Zealand and along the trails of the Blue Ridge Mountains of the South.

Yet despite such exotic and adventuresome off-pavement uses, the all-terrain bike is still used primarily as an all-purpose utility two-wheeler.

The all-terrain or mountain bicycle is by far the most versatile and durable foot-powered vehicle around. It is as at home in the wilds as it is on city streets. Whether you call it mountain biking, all-terrain biking, or by any other name, off-road bicycling is a highly favored form of pedal-powered fun and adventure that is surely here to stay.

2

The Machines

Although it borrows somewhat from touring, cruising, or BMX bicycles, the all-terrain bike is a different breed. It may look like a stripped-down version of the old newsboy clunkers, but appearances deceive. The ATB is designed and assembled to withstand the punishment of off-road action. Yet, for those riders not interested in taking to the backcountry, it provides a comfortable, easygoing ride on any surface.

This means that an all-terrain bike, for all of its ruggedness, must also be lightweight and sprightly. In order to achieve this, such a machine takes a lot of planning, engineering, and skillful assembling of its parts, or *components*. After years of experimenting and testing—punctuated by many crashes, failures, and broken parts—numerous all-terrain bikes have emerged that fill the multi-purpose bill.

The real cornerstone of any bicycle is its frame, for the frame supports all the other parts. Some frames are made of heat-treated aluminum alloy; a few are fabricated of synthetic compounds of one type or another. Most frames, however, are made of steel tubing. For strength and lightness, such steels are usually alloyed with elements such as manganese, vanadium, chromium, or molybdenum. Most quality bicycle frames are made of an alloy known as chrome-molybdenum steel—also referred to as chrome-moly, chromoly, or sometimes simply chro-mo. Chrome-moly lends itself nicely to brazing or welding, the two common methods by which short lengths of round hollow tubing are bonded together to make a frame.

Most bicycle frames are composed of two connected triangles of such tubing, a forward "main frame" and a smaller secondary "rear frame" behind it.

The main frame is made up of three pieces of tubing about 2 feet long. They are a *top tube*, a *down tube*, and a *seat tube*. Seat, handlebar bearings, and pedal mechanism are located at the three corners.

The second triangle, or *rear triangle*, is made up of a pair of parallel *seat stays*, plus a pair of parallel *chain stays* that reach back to hold the rear wheel in place. The seat stays angle downward from the top of the seat tube. The chain stays stretch straight back from

Basic parts of an all-terrain bike. *Peugeot*

the *bottom bracket*, where the pedal mechanism bearings are located. The ends of the two pair of stays are connected by forged *dropouts*. The dropouts contain the slots into which the rear-wheel axle fits.

Both pairs of stays are spread wide enough apart to accommodate the balloon-tired wheel and provide ample clearance for the rear-wheel assembly.

Due to the extra strain put on all-terrain bikes, the frame is generally fabricated of larger and stronger tubing than that normally used on street bikes. Often tubing with an outside diameter of 1¼ inches or 1⅜ inches replaces the more customary 1-inch size. The tubing is often *butted*, which simply means that its wall is made thicker at the end than in the middle. It is called *double-butted* if it is thickened at both ends. Butting adds strength where it is most needed, leaving the area in-between light and flexible. The extra thickness at the ends helps produce strong brazed or welded joints. A smooth continuous bead of brazing or welding material usually indicates a strong joint.

Often *lugs* are used where the frame tubes are joined. Lugging is the practice of slipping a specially designed and often decorative metal sleeve over the connecting tube ends and brazing the joint solidly together.

While the frame is being put together, assorted *braze-ons* are added. Some are small threaded stubs, or *bosses*, used for attaching brakes and derailleurs. Other braze-ons are threaded or drilled to route control cables, hold water-bottle cages, tire pumps, or other bicycling equipment. Screw eyelets are also provided so a biker can add luggage racks, fenders, or other accessories.

An all-terrain bike frame is usually a couple of inches lower and stretched out a bit longer than a typical street or touring bike. This provides a low and stable *center of gravity* for the bike, plus a slightly longer *wheelbase*, or distance between the front- and rear-wheel axle centers. These differences provide a good measure of stability

Good wheels are second only to the frame as the bike's most important components.

and control, two very desirable features in an all-terrain bicycle.

Once a frame has been chosen, wheels are next in order of importance. Wheels of an ATB must be stronger than the thin 27-inch wheels found on most skinny-tired road or touring bicycles. All-terrain bikes generally use 26-inch aluminum-rimmed wheels woven with the usual thirty-six spokes. A few bikers prefer 24-inch wheels. Occasionally small 20-inch BMX wheels are put on all-terrain bikes for younger riders. The smaller wheels of the ATB are not only durable, but keep the center of gravity down low, where it belongs.

Aluminum wheel *rims* are preferable to steel. In wet weather, rubber *brake pads* grip better onto burnished aluminum than onto the more slippery steel. In addition to being lighter than steel and equally strong, aluminum alloys don't rust, which is a decided advantage for any bicycle component.

Wheel hubs of ATBs are usually equipped with sealed bearings to keep out the dirt, water, and mud often encountered in off-road cycling. Bottom bracket and *headset* bearings are also usually sealed to keep them clean and save wear. Sealing also minimizes the need to clean, service, and lubricate the bearings.

All-terrain bike tires must be large to keep from sinking into sand and loose dirt. Balloon tires with a big 2.125-inch cross diameter are commonplace. This size tire puts plenty of tread, or "footprint," on the ground to provide maximum *traction* in dirt. Because the balloon tire holds more than four times the amount of air used in skinny tires, it cushions the bumps.

On the other hand, the big footprint of the balloon tire also creates more road friction, or *rolling resistance*, that holds the bike back. For that reason many all-terrain bikers prefer somewhat smaller diameter tires, such as 26×2.00, 26×1.75, or even a drop down to 26×1.5. These are barely larger than tires on most ten-speed touring cycles. For durability and easy repair, all off-roaders use *clincher* tires with *inner tubes*.

In choosing the tire size, you must consider the type of terrain over which you will be doing most of your riding. Thin tires are fine for hard surfaces. Fatter tires are essential for riding on loose dirt, sand, mud, or even snow.

Off-road tires are usually the bold, knobby-treaded type often seen on the wheels of BMX machines. *Knobbies* provide maximum grip on loose dirt, but on pavement they are inclined to buzz and rumble. To eliminate this, many off-road tires have a smooth center ridge around the outer circumference of the tire. Thus, on pavement, the tire rolls smoothly on the raised ridge. When off-road, the side nubs grip any loose dirt. Such combination tires are preferred for general ATB riding.

Perhaps the next consideration is the bicycle's *drivetrain*. The drivetrain is made up of a forward *crankset* that is linked to a rear sprocket *cluster* by the chain. The whole thing is operated by a pair of pedals located on the ends of rotating *crank arms*. It is all geared to turn the back wheel. On all-terrain bikes the crankset is usually made up of three different-sized *chainrings*, or *chainwheels*. Each chainring has a different number of teeth, which is how the sprocket sizes are measured. A typical grouping of ATB chainrings may consist of 3 separate sprockets with the smallest having 24 teeth, the middle rimmed with 34 teeth, and the largest or outside chainring with 46 teeth. Another triple chainwheel set may have twenty-eight, thirty-eight, and forty-eight teeth. There are wide choices to fit one's tastes and purposes.

The bike's chain-operated drivetrain.

Three-toothed chainrings and sealed bottom bracket bearings are common on all-terrain bikes.

The rear sprocket cluster usually has 5- or 6-toothed *cogs* of different sizes. The cog cluster is part of a *freewheel*, having pawls that allow the bike to coast when not being pedaled. The freewheel quickly engages the rear sprockets when pedaling resumes, reactivating the drivetrain.

A typical 6-sprocket cluster may have a nest of sprockets with 13, 15, 17, 21, 25, and 30 teeth. If you combine a chainwheel having 3 chainrings with a 5- or 6-cog freewheel, you have 15 or 18 speeds to choose from. As we'll see later, it is unlikely that you will use all of the speeds available to you, but they are there.

On all-terrain bikes, where steady low speeds are more important than high racing speeds, the chainrings are generally smaller in size than those on road bikes. The rear cogs of off-road bikes are generally about the same as on street bikes, or even a bit larger in size. Thus, by using, say, the smallest chainring with one of the largest cogs, you shift into what are called low, or *granny gears*.

Granny gears produce a high-powered but low-speed *gear ratio* that enables you to creep up any surface that's not so steep it causes the rear tire to lose traction and spin uselessly in the dirt.

On the other hand, by shifting the chain to a larger chainring and one of the smaller cogs you can move to the high gear combinations needed for speed. But with gears set for speed, you lose much hill-climbing power, and your legs will soon ache with the strain of pedaling.

You obtain the various combinations of gearing by using the front and rear derailleurs. Both of these intricate mechanisms are de-signed to move or shift the chain from one chainring or rear-sprocket cog to another. On all-terrain bikes you do this with hand-operated levers located conveniently on the handlebars, just inside the grips. The *thumb shifters* operate flexible *cables* to activate the individual derailleurs according to your choice of low, medium, or high gear ratios.

The big advantage of thumb shifters over the customary levers mounted on a bike frame is that you don't have to remove your hands from the handlebars to do the shifting. And keeping a firm grip on the handlebars is important to rough off-road cycling, where steering control is a constant concern.

Propelling the bike with its pedal-powered drivetrain is the major function of bicycling. Yet it is almost as important to be able to slow it down or stop it. Other than a few so-called single-speed machines with coaster brakes, and still fewer that use complicated disc brakes, practically all all-terrain bikes use some kind of rim-friction brakes to check their momentum. Off-road brakes are similar to the brakes used on most ten-speed road bikes, but have heavy-duty mechanisms. Instead of the simple caliper-type brakes that have been used for decades on lightweight touring bikes, all-terrain bikers adopted a more durable and positive *cantilever brake* with a reliable *centerpull* cable operation and larger brake pads. Often oversized motorcycle *brake levers* are used. Thus the off-road rider

Most gear changing is done through the rear derailleur and sprocket cogs.

has ample braking power for any terrain. Front and rear brakes are customarily mounted on the *forks* and rear seat stays.

Now, however, another style of brake called the *roller-cam* has taken over the braking chores for many top-grade ATBs. The control cable of a roller-cam brake operates a wedge-shaped cam that squeezes the brake pads hard against the wheel rim with a couple of pulleylike rollers. The roller-cam brake also has an added advantage: its entire mechanism clings close to the wheel. It has no protruding levers or arms to snag the underbrush or get bent or broken in a fall or crash. This is important, for, like derailleurs, off-road bicycle brakes are susceptible to damage when riding is rough—which it often is. Usually the roller-cam brake is mounted the same as a cantilever brake. However, its design makes it possible to mount the rear roller-cam down under the chain stays and out of the way. The main handicap in this position is that a brake located that low tends to collect mud, twigs, or other trail debris.

Steering is a critical function of any bike, and even more so of off-road machines that must maneuver over terrain more suited to mountain goats than wheeled vehicles. The front forks, the handlebars, and the *handlebar stem* or *gooseneck* that connects them to the inside of the *head tube* make up the bike's steering system. All-terrain bike forks are not unlike the forks of other bikes, except that they may be slightly shorter, more ruggedly built, and sometimes have the lower tips bent or raked forward a little more than on most skinny-tired road bikes. The rake of the forks cushions the ride and stretches out the wheelbase a bit, providing additional stability and control.

The unique handlebars are one of the features that make it easy to identify an all-terrain bike. They are loosely described as "flat bars," as opposed to the downturned or "dropped" bars of road and touring bicycles. Flat handlebars with easy-to-reach rubber or plastic foam grips enable a rider to sit upright in a better position not only to survey the trail ahead but also to enjoy the passing scenery,

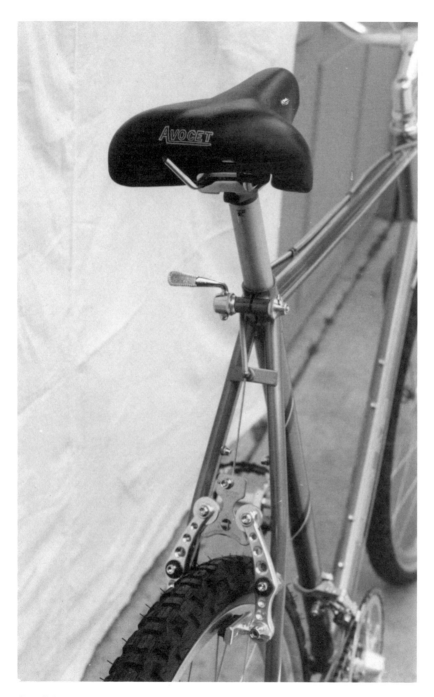

A quick-release seat post, below which is a roller-cam brake.

Straight handlebars anchor the control center of an all-terrain bike. This bike has centerpull cantilever brakes.

which is a large part of what backcountry biking is about.

The flat handlebars are ruggedly built to withstand sudden collisions or tumbles. Some all-terrain bike handlebars are one-piece, triangular-shaped assemblies with the bars and the forked braces and the *stem* welded together in a single unit. Although very strong, these so-called "bullmoose bars" cannot be tilted. They can be adjusted for height only, by raising or lowering the stem in the head tube.

More practical and popular are the two-piece flat handlebar sets in which the straight, or nearly straight, handlebars and stem are separate pieces. Although these bars are gripped firmly in the stem clamp, they can easily be rotated or adjusted by loosening a few

Allen bolts. And, if bent or damaged in any way, the bar can be completely removed from the stem and repaired.

A *saddle* and the pedal assembly round out the functional parts of the all-terrain bike. The saddle may be leather, vinyl, or a similarly durable and comfortable material. The off-road seat is wider and considerably softer than a racing saddle. It may have springs for extra ease. It can be adjusted several inches forward or backward to put you in comfortable reach of the handlebars. Since all-terrain biking often requires saddle adjustments before maneuvering uphill or down, the post that slips into the seat tube should be longer than normal. The long *seat post* provides a wide range of up and down positions and helps compensate for the small all-terrain bike frame.

For rapid changes of saddle height, all-terrain bikes usually have a *quick-release* clamp at the top of the seat tube to make tightening or releasing the pressure on the seat post easier. Some saddle mechanisms even have a compression-spring seat return that automatically raises when you release the clamp and lift your weight off the saddle. Then, to secure the saddle in your favored position, you simply reach down, tighten the quick-release again, and continue on your way.

The all-terrain bike's crank arms are extra strong to endure the strain of climbing hills and the generally rough riding conditions. Long cranks increase pedal leverage, while short cranks provide better ground clearance; choice is by personal preference. To be on the safe side, most all-terrain bikers use normal-length cranks within the 6- or 7-inch range, in the neighborhood of 170 millimeters.

Pedals are usually the sharply edged *rattrap* style found on most BMX cycles. They have toothed edges to grip a riding shoe. ATB pedals are not likely to have straps or *toe clips*. In off-road biking, where you often need to thrust, or *dab*, your feet to the ground to prevent a spill, you can't afford to have your feet bound to the pedals with straps or clips. However, some all-terrain bikers do use toe

A jumble of all-terrain bikes at rest.

clips and even straps when riding in competition. Some, for special reasons of their own, even put drop handlebars instead of straight bars on their off-road bikes. There is no firm standard of just what makes up an all-terrain bike.

With all of the components in place and operating on sealed bearings, the all-terrain bike becomes a versatile pedal-powered machine. It is, indeed, an excellent go-anywhere bicycle.

3

Choosing Your Bike

∫ince all-terrain bicycling makes great demands on both
rider and machine, it is important that you and the bicycle
form a smoothly functioning unit.

You may be able to find a decent enough off-road bike at a
hardware, chain store, or discount house and simply ride it home or
hit the mountain trails with it. Usually it pays to shop around and
compare.

Unless you really know what you are looking for in an all-terrain
bike, you probably would be wise to go to an established bicycle
shop where you can find a large variety of bikes to choose from.
Bike shops sometimes offer used bikes for sale, and you may find a
bargain. Bike shop personnel are usually qualified to help you make
a smart choice. Also, a dealer who operates a fully equipped bike
shop and is an expert repairman may be a valuable friend later on
when you experience bent forks, broken spokes, balky derailleurs,
and other cycling crises.

You can find all-terrain bikes for rent at many bike shops, as well
as campgrounds and other recreational areas. Renting enables you
to try before you buy.

All-terrain bicycles of good to superior quality can cost anywhere
from around $200 to more than $2,000. You will want to choose the

Before buying your all-terrain bike, shop and compare.

strongest, lightest bike best suited for the type of use you intend to give it, at a price you can afford.

If you are the average cyclist you will undoubtedly use your all-terrain bike much more on the pavement than in the dirt. Statistics indicate that some 85 to 90 percent of ATB riding is done on hard surfaces. Mostly the riding takes place on the paved streets of the nation's towns and cities, and on the better country roads. The advantage of having a fat-tire bike is that, in addition to street riding, you can use it on rocky trails, cow paths, dry river bottoms, and other places where a skinny-tired machine would self-destruct. So, in choosing an all-terrain bike, you want to take versatility into account. Consider first what you should look for in a bike that is "dirt-worthy," knowing that if it can handle rough trail riding, it will have no trouble serving as a street or city bike.

There are a great many reliable all-terrain bikes being marketed by such companies as Redline, Specialized, Bike Nashbar, Fisher, Raleigh, Cannondale, Schwinn, Trek, Nishiki, Moot, and Ross, to name some of them. And there are many moderately priced, mass-produced department-store brands manufactured by such established bicycle factories as Huffy, Murray, and Hutch, some of which are also found in bike shops. Your bicycle dealer can guide you to the best brand of brakes, the most dependable derailleurs, the most durable tires, the proper size chainrings, and other important components that make up your machine.

You may need a little help in choosing a proper frame. Some of the top-quality steel frame and fork tubing material is manufactured by Reynolds, Tange, Columbus, and Ishiwata. Usually an identifying decal is stuck on the frame to designate the type of steel and whether or not it is butted for extra strength and lightness. And don't ignore aluminum; some very good lightweight aluminum frames are on the market.

The first measure for fitting yourself to an all-terrain bike is to stand flat-footed astride the frame. There should be between 2 and

3 inches of clearance between you and the top tube. This is an inch or so more than is customary for a skinny-tire road bike. The lower top tube makes it easy to get on and off the bike, and helps prevent you from banging the inside of your thighs when standing up and pedaling vigorously, or "honking," as road racers call it.

To compensate for the lower top tube, all-terrain bikes have an extra long seat post. With the quick-release mechanism, you can easily adjust the saddle for maximum comfort. On an all-terrain bike the most comfortable position of the seat is usually about level with the handlebar grips.

Although the top tube of an ATB frame should be lower than average, the bottom bracket should be higher off the ground, closer to 12 inches than the 10½ or 11 inches for most street bikes. In off-road riding, the extra bottom bracket height allows clearance for maneuvering over rocks, logs, or other trail debris. It also helps prevent pedals from digging into the ground when cornering a sharp turn.

The size of a bike frame is measured by the distance from the middle of the bottom bracket to the top of the seat tube. On an all-terrain bike this may range anywhere from 17 to 23 inches. Since the top tube is lower and the bottom bracket higher, you usually use a smaller-size frame for an all-terrain bike than you would a road or touring machine. You make whatever fine height adjustments you need by raising or lowering the saddle and handlebars.

You must be careful that the top tube is not so long that it puts the straight handlebars out of easy reach. Nor should it be so short that your legs are cramped or knock against the handlebars when turning. Although you can make some adjustments by sliding the saddle forward or back on its tracks, you shouldn't rely on it. Start out by choosing a frame that is most comfortable when everything is in "neutral."

Whether you intend to ride on pavement or in dirt, try to keep your all-terrain bike's weight below 30 pounds. This is not always

Standing astride the bike, there should be 2–3 inches of clearance between the rider and the frame.

easy, particularly on less-expensive bikes where heavy-gauge ordinary steel tubing is used instead of the lighter, double-butted chrome-moly or aluminum. Steel rims, cranksets, and other heavy metal components made of steel instead of lighter and equally durable aluminum alloys add more weight. Plus, all off-road bikes use balloon tires of one size or another, and balloon tires weigh more than skinny tires.

For riding off-road you should keep your bike simple and stripped of unnecessary accessories. However, since most riding of ATBs is actually done around town on hard-surfaced streets, you may want some extra comforts and conveniences. You can put on fenders or splash shields. You can add luggage racks for toting things, or a chain guard to protect your pants legs. A variety of accessories are available. It's a good idea to always carry a bicycle pump. Lightweight and clamped out of the way on one of the frame tubes, the tire pump can save the day for you. The better pumps fit either Schrader or Presta tire valve stems. Be sure the pump matches the valve.

Vehicle and safety codes usually require lights and reflectors on any bikes that are ridden after dark. It is both foolish and dangerous not to abide by such sensible rulings.

Most off-road bikes come without a *kickstand*. Indeed, a kickstand does tend to rattle and may become jarred out of place when you are bumping over rutted trails or racing over a moto course. However, you often have a parking problem when you don't have a kickstand. You could lay your bike on the ground or find something to lean it against, but neither is a very good choice. A kickstand simplifies the parking problem.

So equip your bike for whatever type of riding you intend to do most of the time. If you use it occasionally for off-road adventuring or competition, you can always strip it down to its "fighting weight."

Choose your brakes carefully; if they should fail while charging down a steep winding trail, you become an instant candidate for

For city riding you may want to add a rack, kickstand, lock, and other conveniences usually left off stripped-down dirt bikes.

splints or plaster casts. Both centerpull cantilever brakes or the roller-cam variety are reliable. As a rule, you can accept the brakes that come on your bike. But brakes are sometimes interchangeable, and advice from your bicycle dealer could be valuable. Be sure your all-terrain bike comes equipped with sufficiently strong brake levers and control cables that are heavy enough to eliminate any stretch or spongy feeling when you squeeze down on the brakes. Often the same heavy-duty brake cables and control levers that are used on motorcycles are adapted to all-terrain bicycles. Shimano, Dia-Compe, SunTour, and Tomaselli are among the better brake component manufacturers.

It is a good idea to carry an extra set of rubber brake pads with you. Although all-terrain bike brake blocks are oversized and heavier than touring brake pads on the so-called skinny bikes, trail riding is extremely hard on brakes. Wise riders replace pads before they get badly worn.

You should pay particular attention to your bike's drivetrain, for this is the mechanism of pedals, sprockets, and chain that actually propels your bike. The drivetrain not only converts muscle power to wheel power, but, through your skillful operation, enables you to go just about anyplace you want, no matter how difficult.

You should pay extra attention to the quality of derailleurs used on your off-road bike. The derailleurs are the most sensitive and perhaps the most important components on your machine. When ridden off-road, all-terrain bike derailleurs are subject to much more abuse than the gear shifters on street bikes. Weeds and twigs can become entangled in them. Dirt and mud foul them. They are easily bent and knocked out of alignment. You can fine-tune the shifting mechanism with adjusting screws, but you must learn the knack. This is usually explained in the owner's manual that comes with the bike. But, with the exception of simple adjustments, correcting most derailleur problems is best left to an expert bicycle mechanic.

All of the moving parts of an all-terrain bike operate on four main

With care, you can fine-tune your derailleur.

sets of ball bearings, the best of which are sealed bearings. They are located in the front and rear hubs, in the bottom bracket assembly, and in the steering headset. You need good, long-lasting bearings on your bike or you won't get anywhere.

So your primary concerns when choosing an all-terrain bike are the frame, the drivetrain, the brakes, derailleurs, and major moving parts. You also must pick a comfortable saddle, pedals to fit your biking shoes, and assorted other levers, handlebars, and controls necessary for operating the bike.

Keep in mind that there are squeaks, grinds, and rattles that you generally don't hear until you are pedaling along some road or backcountry trail. So don't be afraid to shake and jounce the bike around a little while still in the bike shop, just in case something is already loose or improperly assembled.

Having considered all things and checked them out, you should sense what to look for in an all-terrain bike. You should end up with an all-terrain bike that will meet whatever street or off-road riding demands you make of it.

It's a big beginning—but just a beginning. It takes more than a bicycle to become a skilled off-road cyclist.

4

Getting Ready

Once you have your all-terrain bike, you will undoubtedly be anxious to put it through its paces. Chances are that you already know how to ride a bike, and with any skill at all in bicycling, you will have no trouble adapting to your ATB. Despite some differences, an off-road bicycle is still a collection of wheels, pedals, handlebars, chains, and ball bearings put together in an almost standard fashion.

The main distinction is in some of the things you do on a fat-tire all-terrain bike that you wouldn't dare attempt on a skinny-tired road bike. So you have to prepare both physically and mentally for the new experience in bicycling.

A good place to start is with your clothing. You probably will do most of your ATB riding in the same clothes you wear for your other daily activities. There certainly is nothing wrong with pedaling around the neighborhood in jeans, a T-shirt, and scruffy tennis shoes. Shorts are all right if you are willing to risk getting sunburned or scratched by branches or thorns. The same risks go with short-sleeved shirts. So ride in whatever clothes you feel comfortable, and whichever clothes protect you from minor hazards. You will do fine riding to school, commuting to work, or simply pedaling around town in clothes of your choice.

No matter what else you wear, a helmet is your best insurance

A group of off-road bikers gather for an outing.

against injury—and head injuries are by far any cyclist's greatest concern. You should wear a hard-shell helmet that meets or exceeds the performance criteria established by the American National Standards Institute (ANSI). Considerably smaller and lighter than motorcycling helmets, ANSI-approved biking helmets can nonetheless absorb a great deal of shock and prevent a serious head injury in the event of a fall or an accident.

A proper helmet is made of a rigid impact-resistant outer shell with a snug-fitting polystyrene foam inner liner. Usually the helmet has vents to allow warm air to escape and cool air to enter. It should also have a sturdy quick-release chin strap, and perhaps a sun visor. You can pick your color. Keep in mind that it's usually wise to choose a color that is bright and easily visible.

The importance of wearing an approved helmet cannot be overemphasized. Since 1986, the National Off-Road Bicycle Association

(NORBA), the governing body for organized all-terrain bicycle competition, and the United States Cycling Federation (USCF) that controls amateur skinny-tire bicycling affairs have made wearing a hard-shell helmet mandatory in all of their *sanctioned* events. Often local or state laws require that protective helmets be worn when you ride on public roads. The helmets are just as important in the backcountry. Years ago most cyclists wore caps or other soft, nonprotective headgear. Some radically bold cyclists who began wearing helmets were considered a bit overcautious. Not anymore. Helmets have saved too many bicycle pedalers from serious head injury or, indeed, death, to be ignored. A sturdy helmet is now the mark of a sensible and experienced cyclist. It is not only essential, but very much in style. Wear one!

Hard-shell helmets protect against head injuries.

Although many ATB owners ride in ordinary street clothes, some serious off-road bikers who venture into remote areas or go on longer trips wear colorful and durable clothing similar to that chosen by millions of ten-speed road touring bicyclists. As an all-terrain biker, you must dress not only for comfort and the weather but, if your dirt trail leads through thick brush country, you must plan protection for your arms and legs. Thus, many times it is wise to wear long sleeves, long pants, gloves, and other safeguards.

Today's specialized cycling clothing is designed for both style and function. Although black had long been favored for cycling shorts, they now come in all colors, as do other clothing items. There are several things to consider when choosing your riding clothes. They should be close-fitting enough to minimize wind drag and be comfortable in all areas, and they should allow full freedom of movement. Avoid loose, baggy clothes that could bunch up, catch air, or become caught in the moving parts of your bike. Machine-washable synthetics are favored.

Shorts are usually fabricated of a blend of nylon and Lycra four-way stretch synthetic material that fits snugly to the contours of your body and allows you to pedal freely. The legs stretch to mid-thigh, knee-length, or sometimes are full ankle length. However, all but the briefest shorts help to prevent a rider's legs from chafing against the saddle or top tube. For cold weather you probably will prefer the full-length, form-fitting wool, nylon, or polypropylene tights. Many shorts or tights have removable seat inserts made of washable chamois skin, or a thin foamlike synthetic cushioning for comfort in the saddle area. Depending upon how rough the riding, knees and hips may be padded for extra protection. Some cyclists wear thermal suits, gaiters, or booties for added warmth in cool weather.

Your next consideration should be your jersey. Whether you choose short or long sleeves will depend on the terrain over which you ride, your inclination to perspire, and, of course, the weather

Good bike wear is both stylish and functional.

you are likely to encounter. Some jerseys have pockets in the back instead of the front to keep whatever small items you may be carrying out of the way.

It is wise to have a windbreaker available, and a lightweight rain poncho or cape can be a handy item when you are ten miles from home and a storm comes boiling over the hills. These things can all be carried in a seat- or handlebar pack, or in panniers that attach to your rear bike rack.

Gloves are a good addition to your bicycling wardrobe. There are many types. Most have soft terry cloth or mesh backing, mainly for ventilation, but they are also handy for wiping the sweat from your face. The palm area is leather and is padded for comfort and secure gripping and also to help absorb the road shock and vibrations that travel up through the handlebars. Usually the glove fingers are cut off just above the knuckles to provide a good bare-fingered feel for delicate riding. Gloves protect your hands in a crash and from thorny bushes, too. They reduce palm pressure on the handlebars and help delay finger numbness on a long ride. Buy your gloves plenty snug; they stretch with use. A pair of safety sunglasses offer additional protection. They are essential when you ride in brush country.

A pair of decent riding shoes aids pedaling. There is nothing wrong with tennis shoes or some of the assorted running or training shoes that are so popular and inexpensive. However, the soles should be fairly thick and stiff to distribute the foot pressure evenly on the pedals, yet soft enough to hold securely to the serrated edges of the rattrap pedals found on most all-terrain bikes. Some

Any shoe that will hold to the serrated edges of the rattrap pedals will do.

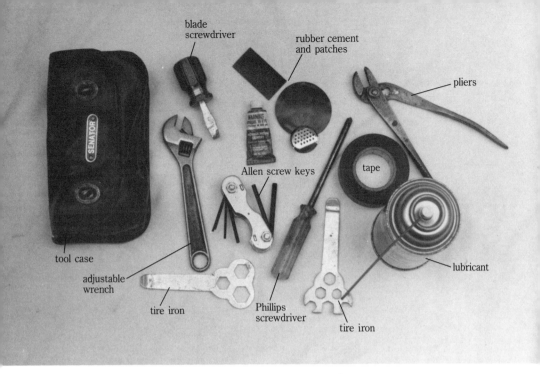

blade
screwdriver

rubber cement
and patches

pliers

SENATOR

Allen screw keys

tape

tool case

lubricant

adjustable
wrench

tire iron

Phillips
screwdriver

tire iron

A few simple tools will handle most minor bike problems.

bicycling shoes have grooves molded into the soles that help grip
the pedals in rough riding conditions. But the special cleated shoes
often used by road racers and ten-speed touring cyclists are of no
use to all-terrain bikers who frequently have to dab their feet to the
ground to prevent a spill. Lightweight waffle-treaded hiking shoes
are appropriate, since backcountry cycling frequently requires that
you dismount and push or portage your bike over or around some
hill or obstacle.

Just be sure your shoes are comfortable and well ventilated. A
pair of good sport socks will help also.

Aside from a few items of extra clothing you might take along to
protect yourself from the elements, there are assorted things you
should carry to help you through possible emergencies.

You will need to carry a few basic tools to take care of repairs.
Besides a screwdriver and bicycle *tire irons*, you should have a pair
of pliers, a 6-inch adjustable wrench, and perhaps several appropri-

All-terrain biking and camping go well together. *Don Neumeier*

ate sizes of the six-sided L-shaped *Allen wrench* keys to fit the sunken heads of the bolts holding various assemblies together. A small roll of duct or friction tape and a yard or so of plain old wire could come in mighty handy in a pinch. Never be caught far from home without a tire-patching kit. And don't forget the extra brake pads. You can tie the whole collection up in a rag that can also be used to clean up your bike and your hands after you have made your field repairs.

For yourself, carry a small first-aid kit with a few Band-Aids, some adhesive tape, sunburn cream, and a few simple survival items. All of this will fit nicely into a small handlebar pouch or seat pack.

That should do it, unless you're heading out on a long trip or a weekend jaunt. Then you had better think of food, water, a map, a sleeping bag, and perhaps a small tent of some kind. All told, for a long trip you may end up with 30 to 40 pounds of assorted supplies. Packing for convenience, safety, and comfort is an art in itself. But, if you have patience and use common sense, you will learn to pack your supplies in the order that you will need to get to them. If you keep the weight down low for stability and distribute the load, you will hardly be aware of it. You probably won't get it right the first time, but with practice you can acquire this valuable skill.

All bicycling depends upon your physical well-being and muscle control. Of course, some types of bicycling are more demanding than others. You can pedal leisurely down the street to school without expending much energy. For that type of biking you won't need to prepare ahead of time. But off-road biking makes excessive demands on your physical strength and skills. It is good to prepare

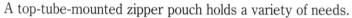

A top-tube-mounted zipper pouch holds a variety of needs.

yourself to withstand the strain and to keep up with others who may have quietly and sensibly kept in shape.

If you are a bit overweight, bicycling is a great way to slim down and get your muscles in shape. To bicycle properly you do more than hang on to the handlebars, sit in the saddle, and let your leg muscles do the work. You put your whole being into the effort. You distribute the load between the legs, arms, and body. This helps prevent exhausting any particular set of muscles prematurely, although you can be sure that the leg and thigh muscles will be the first to complain.

So, to get and stay lean, wiry, and healthy, as most good cyclists are, you should watch what you eat. Go easy on greasy foods, because fat is hard to digest and does not provide the type of energy you need for strenuous action.

You are better off eating carbohydrates, which put out more durable long-lasting muscle fuel called glycogens. These are generally found in starchy foods such as bread, macaroni, and potatoes. At least half your meals should lean toward the carbohydrates. You should get the bulk of the remaining calories from protein such as is found in fish, chicken, lean meat, and nonfat milk. Also add the nonfattening energy you can get from the vegetables and fruits. If you eat sensibly, you are on the right track not only for good cycling, but for a healthy, long life. Eating wisely comes down to using common sense. In normal riding you burn up about 30 calories per mile, or 800 calories per hour, depending upon how hard and fast you are pedaling. Eat lightly before you ride. For long rides take an extra banana or two to help stoke the body furnace. A candy bar provides quick energy. Always start out with full water bottles to stave off the dehydration caused by profuse sweating.

If you are a serious cyclist, or are starting out on a lengthy ride, you should warm up before hitting the road or trail. Do some simple body bends and torso twists. Touch your toes a few times. Rotate your head. Arch your back. Do what any sensible athlete does to

Take plenty of liquids to make up for perspiration loss.

Stretch and loosen up before starting out on a strenuous ride.

prepare himself or herself for competition. Get your body and limbs in supple working order. It will help keep you from cramping up or pulling a muscle, which can happen if you try getting under way too soon and too fast.

To set the bike up for maximum riding comfort and efficiency, you should adjust the saddle height by sliding it up or down in the seat tube. When the pedal is at its lowest point and you put the heel of your foot on it, your leg should be straight. Then, when you shift the ball of your foot to the pedal in proper riding position, it puts a slight bend in your knee. In this position you can extend your leg properly and pedal comfortably without cramping or overstretching.

To fine-tune the saddle, level or tilt it to the most comfortable position. Slide it forward or back in its track so that you can reach

Correct saddle height leaves a slight bend at the knee when the pedal is down.

the handlebar grips without stretching or crowding your arms. You should have complete freedom of movement, and your pumping knees should never interfere with your hands or arms or come into contact with any part of the bike. You should be able to reach your brake levers and thumb shifters without having to remove your hands from the grips.

Now that you are helmeted, dressed for comfort and safety, and have adjusted your bike, you are ready to go. Just remember that whether you will be cruising the neighborhood, sweating your way up a rutted, leg-numbing hill, or slogging hub-deep through an icy stream, the reason you have an all-terrain bike is to have fun.

5

Street Riding

most of the time you will probably use your all-terrain bike for activity less strenuous than panting up a steep rock-strewn slope or hurtling down a dirt drop-off. A fine all-purpose machine, your all-terrain bike will do virtually anything that any other bike will do, plus it has the sturdiness to operate over rough terrain that would promptly destroy a skinny-tired lightweight machine. And, due to its stability and extra ruggedness, your all-terrain bike will give you fewer problems. With the heavy-duty balloon tires, you will have fewer punctures and blowouts. You will experience less frequent part failures because the components that make up the bike are stronger.

You may find that your all-terrain bike won't whisk you where you're going quite as fast as a more sprightly ten-speed lightweight, but the slight edge you may give up in speed you make up for in comfort. The soft and broad seat, the more cushiony tires, and the upright sitting position that straight handlebars encourage provide for a more pleasant, sight-seeing ride than you normally get when hunched over the dropped handlebars of a skinny-tired speedster. Even with an all-terrain bike, if you really want extra speed you need only spin the pedals faster or shift into a high gear.

So, enjoy yourself around town by using your all-terrain bicycle as a convenient mode of transportation. To get the most pleasure

All-terrain bikes are used mainly for simple neighborhood riding.

and efficiency out of your ride, set your bike up properly ahead of time, as described earlier.

For street riding you should inflate your tires to thumb-resisting hardness. The larger the tire the less pressure is needed to firm it up. Balloon tires with 2.125- or 2-inch diameters will normally take 35 to 50 psi (pounds per square inch), although some city riders will try more. But to overinflate your tires is to flirt with blowouts.

Generally, the smaller the tire the more pressure you can safely put into it.

Many off-road riders prefer small 1.75-inch or even 1.50-inch clincher-type tires with appropriate inner tubes for pavement riding. If you keep them firmly inflated, less rubber hits the ground and there is less road friction. Hard tires do not make a soft ride, but they do make pedaling easier.

For city biking dress for the weather, destination, and occasion. Most anything goes that is comfortable and doesn't bind, chaff, or catch in the moving parts. Since all-terrain bikes do not ordinarily have chain guards, pants legs are easily chewed up in the chain-wheel sprockets. You can roll up the cuffs, slip rubber bands over them, or use those classic inexpensive spring clips that have been around for a hundred years.

Above all, remember that an approved hard-shell helmet is your best and least expensive insurance against serious injury.

Before starting out, it's a good idea to "preflight" your bike. Check carefully for loose nuts, bolts, or anything that squeaks, rattles, or grinds. You'll do no harm by spraying a bit of bicycle lubricant on the chain and other exposed moving parts. But do it sparingly and wipe off the excess so it won't collect dust and grime or contaminate the brake pad contact surface of the rim.

If you always carry your small basic tool kit, you will be set for tightening things and making small repairs wherever and whenever they occur—which is usually at a most inconvenient time and place.

Bicycling on city streets involves a different set of concerns than you are faced with while off-road riding on some backcountry trail. Call them rules of the road or laws of self-preservation. By any name, they are critical to your well-being. Statistics indicate that an average bicyclist is apt to have an accident of some sort about every two years. But if you are a careful and sensible rider you stay comfortably on the lower and safer end of that average. Most biking accidents result in minor bruises, abrasions, or cuts. About one out

Street wear is fine for general freestyle action, but wear a helmet.

of fifty requires a doctor's attention. Tragically, for about a thousand bicyclists a year in the United States it is too late for doctors.

Automobiles constitute a city cyclist's greatest threat. In any given year close to 100,000 accidents involving automobiles and bicycles occur on American roads. So it makes good sense when you are out bicycling to avoid automobiles whenever possible. In order to do this, you should stay off heavily traveled streets and boulevards. Use the less-traveled side streets. Not only is travel safer there, but the air is cleaner and the scenery is usually superior to that on traffic-clogged thoroughfares.

As far as the law is concerned, a bicycle on the street is a vehicle just the same as a truck, bus, car, motorcycle, moped, or motor scooter. Although as a bicyclist you aren't usually required to register your bike or to have a driver's license, you must be aware of and abide by the same rules that apply to all motor vehicles. If you are wise you will pay strict attention to those rules. You are the smallest and most vulnerable piece of moving machinery on the street. You will be no match for any of the other vehicles. You are a sardine swimming in a sea of gasoline-powered sharks.

It's not that automobile drivers are out to get you. They aren't. But they are driving a ton or so of rapidly moving metal that is difficult to maneuver quickly, and still more difficult to stop. Knowing this, you had better always be on the defensive. Keep your eye out for trouble, and stop or get out of the way the moment you see it coming. Keep your head on a swivel, checking around yourself at all times. If you follow the rules of the road, stay alert, and think ahead, you should be able to avoid accidents.

One rule of the road gives a pedestrian the right-of-way over the cyclist, so you must always yield to the man or woman afoot on street, sidewalk, or path. On the other hand, although you may technically have the right-of-way over a pickup truck approaching an intersection from your left, you should not insist upon exercising it. Play it safe. You are outweighed and overmatched. Be smart—give way and let him pass.

You must recognize and obey all traffic lights and signs. Respect stop signs. Don't fudge. Come to a full stop and look both ways before you proceed. A rolling stop will only get you into trouble if a car comes charging around a blind corner or makes a sudden turn in front of you. Most bicycle-automobile collisions happen when the cyclist noses too soon into or across the flow of traffic.

Keep far to the right side of the road. At the same time, pay attention to a soft shoulder or a gravel ridge that might cause you to skid or flip. Always ride with the flow of traffic, not against it. This enables you to look ahead and plan your progress defensively. Also, it provides the driver behind you with the chance to judge your movements and give you plenty of clearance. Besides, riding with the flow of traffic is the law.

Give proper hand signals. Left arm straight out indicates your intention to make a left turn. Elbow bent and left hand pointing up signals a right turn. Left arm down and out with palm turned to the rear means you are slowing down or stopping. In any case, even when giving proper signals, be sure you are clear in all directions before starting your maneuver.

Stay out of the middle of the street, unless you are preparing to make a left turn. This is one of a cyclist's more risky movements, since it puts you right in the middle of the traffic, so be particularly cautious. If there is much traffic, you are better off if you stay to the right, dismount at the intersection, and walk your bike over the crosswalk with other pedestrians.

Switching lanes, swerving, veering, or weaving in and out of traffic causes most accidents on city streets. Don't do it. Ride a steady, straight course. Save the stunts and fancy stuff for another time and a safer place.

Stop at railroad crossings when the signal is flashing. Stop also for school buses. Stop for fire engines, ambulances, police cars, or other emergency vehicles that are flashing red lights or sounding sirens.

Keep your all-terrain bike fairly stripped down and lightweight. Lightness gives the all-terrain bike the sprightliness that helps make riding ATBs so much fun. Of course, there are times when you may want to load your bike down with assorted supplies. Only you can determine what you need to carry on your short or long bicycling trips.

You should never try to carry a passenger on your all-terrain

Give proper hand signals when riding on city streets.

Save curb-jumping freestyling for quiet side streets.

bike, either on the handlebars or riding side-saddle on the top tube. This is indeed a hazardous practice. A passenger throws everything out of balance. Unless you have front or rear racks on your bike, you must also be careful when hauling packages. A hand-carried package or one loosely balanced on the handlebars is sure to cause serious loss of bike control—a bad situation at any time, and doubly so in traffic.

All of the precautionary measures that apply to any type of

metropolitan street bicycling should be practiced by all-terrain bikers as well, because the only difference is in the style of bike you ride. Always be aware of what is going on around you. Be tuned in on the sound of approaching motors, the direction of the wind, a dog's bark, and anything else that warns of impending action that might affect the operation of your bike.

Survey the road ahead for an unfilled pothole, a gaping crack in the pavement, a slotted grating, or inlaid railroad tracks. Be careful on wet pavement. Watch out for sand, gravel, or clumps of wet leaves, any one of which can cause a nasty fall.

You must not ride your bike on a freeway, expressway, turnpike, most toll roads, or major highways. Streets that can be ridden on usually provide a bicycle lane and are posted with signs warning other types of vehicles. Stay in the bicycle lane; it is there to protect you from the threat of high-density, high-speed traffic.

If you ride after dark, you need more than a reflector. You must have a headlamp that can be seen for at least 500 feet and a tail light or super reflector visible for 300 feet or more to the rear. At night you should wear light-colored clothing or a reflective sash or vest to make you stand out in the view of an approaching motorist. There are assorted beaconlike reflective devices and warning gadgets that can be worn by a person or attached to the bike to help maintain a safe distance between bicyclist and motorist. You can check them out at your bike shop.

When cycling with a friend or a group, which is a large part of the fun, always ride single file on any street where there is the least bit of traffic. Stay a couple of bike lengths away from the nearest rider. Keep well to the right. Motorists will give you credit for intelligence and will be extra cooperative.

It should go without saying, but if you are ever tempted to hitch a ride by grabbing onto another moving vehicle—*don't!* It is sheer lunacy. Also be careful passing cars parked at the curb. An unnoticed occupant may suddenly swing the door open in your path.

One manufacturer offers a fold-out whirling beacon that warns motorists to keep a safe distance away. *North American International*

Being the latest thing in two-wheelers, off-road bicycles have become prime targets for thieves. Wherever you park yours, don't forget to lock it. Well over half a million bikes are stolen every year in the United States.

There are two basic types of locks. One popular model comes in the form of a large, armor steel, U-shaped staple with a snap-lock crossbar attached. Attached to wheel, sprocket, or frame, it effectively immobilizes your bike. To prevent a determined thief from hauling your bike away, lock and all, the lock should be large enough to reach around an anchoring object such as a parking meter post, the bar of a bike rack, or another small, fixed object. This style of lock is neatly stowed in a special clip that attaches to the frame of your bicycle. It is available in assorted sizes. Some come with an insurance policy protecting you from loss because of theft, if the lock is used properly.

You may prefer to use a cable-and-lock combination, which is usually made up of a self-coiling 6-foot length of hardened-steel, vinyl-covered cable with end loops. Fastened by a durable tamperproof padlock, such a device makes your bike fairly thief-proof. It has the ability to go around much larger anchoring objects such as fence posts or telephone poles. The long cable and separate lock are a bit unwieldy and awkward to stow when not in use. There are other types of bicycle locks that do a good job. Check around for the

A good lock thwarts thieves.

Doing endos is good practice for bicycle control.

one that best fits your needs. Any lock should be sheathed in vinyl or other cushioning material to protect the fine finish on your bike.

You certainly need not let safety rules and precautionary measures spoil your biking fun. They are meant to enhance your bicycling pleasure. After all, sensible bicyclists the world over have followed such rules for decades.

All city cyclists get the urge now and then to do some *stunting* and try a few tricks on their bikes. Why not? That is part of the fun and challenge of owning a bike. And you can do the tricks on an all-terrain bike that you can do on any other two-wheeler. *Wheelies?* Sure. *Endos?* Of course. Jumping? It's easy on an ATB. And, due to the extra ruggedness of an all-terrain bike, you are not likely to bend a wheel against the curb, or spring the forks if you misjudge your skill a little.

Do these things on side streets where there are no cars, or on some hard-surfaced path. But get the most out of your all-terrain bike.

Yet despite the pleasure you get from riding on concrete or other hard surfaces, the day will surely come when you will want to take your bike out beyond where the pavement ends . . . into the dirt.

6

Backcountry Exploring

I f you own the one and only type of bicycle designed and built to survive the demolishing effects of rough, rocky, and rugged terrain, it is almost inevitable that you will want to take off on jeep trails, sashay your way through sandstone canyons, jostle over forest service roads, logging tracks, and numerous other dirt paths never meant for the frail wheels of ordinary bicycles.

You can set off on an off-road cycling safari alone, or, as is usually preferable and more fun, go with a friend or two, or even join a group. If you don't have acquaintances who go all-terrain biking, look up a group or join a club of touring or off-road adventurers. Your local bicycle shop can tip you off to such a band of cyclers. Your area newspaper may occasionally feature an item about some all-terrain biking event about to take place. Be in touch with other cyclists in your area. Members of NORBA receive a monthly newsletter and events calendar listing everything that's happening in the world of all-terrain bicycling.

Some cyclists live close enough to the wilderness to simply mount their bikes and pedal out beyond the pavement and into the dirt-trailed hills. More than likely, on major explorations you will need to tote your bike in a pickup truck or a vehicle that has some kind of car rack to the site where the off-road action begins. There

A group of young off-road cyclists on a backcountry adventure. *Los Angeles YMCA*

are all kinds of bumper-carriers or roof-mounted bike racks to fit the need.

You must consider where and under what conditions you will do your off-road riding. There is frequently some opposition to anyone trespassing upon the natural state of things—whether it be the

A cartop rack is handy for transporting bikes to a wilderness area. *Don Neumeier*

forest, desert, seashore, riverbed, or mountain slope. And, although a bicycle certainly is less upsetting to the ecology than, say, a jeep, motorcycle, ATV (motorized all-terrain vehicle), or, indeed, a horse, the off-road bike is new to the scene and, therefore, sometimes not fully accepted.

There is no denying that any moving piece of equipment used without precautions can cause environmental damage. Even hikers and backpackers wearing heavy, waffle-treaded boots are sometimes accused of damaging the "forest primeval."

So you must be careful when you encroach upon nature's scheme of things. You can avoid harming plant life simply by staying on trails, dirt roads, firebreaks, or whatever designated routes are open to hikers, equestrians, cyclists, or ATVs of any kind. You can help keep down erosion by staying clear of ruts and minor washouts that early rains may have put in a trail. Cross them at a sharp angle, or jump over them. Don't follow them and intensify the erosion. Don't shortcut switchbacks in the trail; this tends to wear new paths and aggravate erosion.

Don't head off across some verdant meadow or barge through some other fragile ecosystem. Avoid leaving deep, ugly scars when the ground is wet by staying away from soft dirt or clay, both of which quickly turn to mud. Besides, it will only gum up your bike. Keep to the harder rock or shale surfaces. They may give you a rough ride, but roughness is all part of the fun of off-pavement but on-trail bicycling.

It is important to do your off-road riding only in approved areas. Whether public or private land, you generally need permission to ride over it. For instance, at this time millions of acres of the nation's wilderness areas are closed to all "mechanical forms of transport." Naturally, this means jeeps, motorcycles, ATVs, and similar engine-powered vehicles. Until or unless there is a change, it also includes muscle-powered bicycles.

On the other hand, such government agencies as the U.S. Forest Service, the Bureau of Land Management, and the National Park Service control vast networks of trails, logging roads, and service roads. Many parts are open to bicyclists who will abide by a few simple rules designed to protect the environment and not to harass or endanger hikers, backpackers, horseback riders, and others who have long been permitted to use the resources.

However, some parts remain closed to bicycles. Cyclists are generally prohibited from using the trails within the National Park System, which are reserved for foot traffic. However, paved roads and many paths within the parks are usually open to cyclists as well as other vehicles. It is the responsibility of the individual or cycling group to check with the appropriate ranger station, land office, or personnel to determine where off-road bicycling is permitted, and to obtain fire permits where needed.

Certainly, if you want to cycle over private land, you need to get

Many forest paths are open to cyclists. *Don Neumeier*

permission from the owner. If assured that you will be respectful of the terrain, be careful around livestock, and not otherwise become a two-wheeled menace, the owner may welcome you in. Whether he lets you come back will depend on how careful and responsible you have proven to be.

No matter where you do your riding, you should abide by the off-roader's code of conduct, set up by NORBA, so you don't wear out your welcome. Remember, you are the "new kid on the block." You have moved into the domain that has long been enjoyed exclusively by hikers, backpackers, and horseback riders. They may resent your intrusion, so you must try to build your image as a friendly two-wheeled off-roader, even when it may seem inconvenient. Avoid confrontations. When approaching hikers, give an early and congenial warning, and pass with care. Encountering a horse, be particularly careful that you don't do anything to spook it. Some-

When off-road riding, take time to pause and refresh yourself. *Don Neumeier*

times it is best to get off your bike and stand beside the trail to let a skittish horse go by.

Stay on trails and established paths. Control your speed. Approach blind turns cautiously, anticipate meeting someone just around the bend. Don't chase or stampede livestock of any kind. Approach slowly and give animals time to move out of your way—or you move out of theirs. Respect No Trespassing signs. Don't litter. Pack out what you pack in.

Plan ahead for the longer back-road journeys. Carry a map with your planned route traced on it. Expect weather changes, and carry proper protective clothing in your packs or panniers. Leave word with someone detailing where you plan to go and when you intend to return. Lots of unforeseen things can happen in the wilds.

Do these things and, as an all-terrain bicyclist, you become a positive and welcome addition to the world of the outdoors.

Due largely to your straight handlebars, you ride in an upright position. Thus, you can watch the birds, study the passing scenery, stop and smell the flowers, and do all the other things that escape speeding motorists. You may cover ten miles or thirty. You set your own pace.

Whenever plans carry you beyond the city limits, it is wise to carry water, emergency food, and body protection. Although an all-terrain bike is rugged and dependable, a breakdown can turn a day tour into an unexpected overnighter. Be ready, just in case. However, don't take along "everything but the kitchen sink." Only by traveling light can you get the full enjoyment out of off-road exploration.

In tackling the rough country, you need to develop a different set of riding skills than you normally use when pedaling over smooth and level surfaces. To aid in this, your all-terrain bike probably has a chainwheel assembly made up of three separate chainrings attached to the pedals. There are also five or six freewheel cogs at the rear. Both are called sprockets.

A group of healthy and friendly bikers usually have no trouble finding off-road places to explore. *Los Angeles YMCA*

A sprocket's size is measured by the number of teeth it has. The teeth, of course, must fit the standard-size links of the bicycle chain. There are many sizes of chainrings. All-terrain bikes generally use chainrings ranging in size from about twenty-four teeth in the small sprocket to perhaps forty-eight in the largest one. You lose speed but gain climbing power when you use a small chainring.

Freewheel clusters of five or six cogs have from about thirteen to thirty teeth. To be a good rider you must be skilled at choosing the right combination of front and rear sprockets for the gearing combination that best fits each situation.

You needn't get too involved in gearing, but there is a simple formula that gives an idea of what it's all about and how you can benefit from it. Say that you use your bike's medium chainring having thirty-six teeth in combination with a seventeen-tooth rear sprocket or freewheel cog, and your ATB probably has a 26-inch-diameter rear wheel. To work out the ratio, you take the first figure, divide it by the second figure, and multiply the result by the third. It looks like this:

$$\frac{\text{(Teeth in front sprocket or chainring) } 36}{\text{(Teeth in rear sprocket or freewheel) } 17} \times \text{(Wheel size) } 26 = 55.06$$

The 55.06 (round it off to 55) is called the *gear ratio*. Gear ratios are used primarily in making comparisons that help determine what combinations of gears make pedaling easy. Gear ratios ranging from 40 to about 100 are suited to riding on level hard surfaces. In loose dirt or on steep trails, you need lower numbers of, say, around 30 or 35, sometimes even less. The small numbers indicate a low, slow, powerful gear combination, where you have to spin your pedals fast to just creep along or pump up a steep slope. Large numbers indicate high speed or downslope cruising gears. If you know the number of teeth in your various sprockets, and have pencil and paper along, you can easily chart out your gear ratios. Simple printed charts are often available at your local bike shop.

If you are interested in how far you travel for each full revolution of the pedals, you multiply the gear-ratio number—55 in our example—by pi (π), or 3.14. The answer is approximately 173 inches; nearly 14½ feet. You will probably not think about road inches or feet as you are pedaling along some woodland trail, but they do provide a measuring stick by which you can tell what each combination of gears can accomplish.

Most of the time, however, you will do your shifting by feel and habit. You will soon learn not to shift so that you use the large outside chainring in combination with the large inside rear cog. Or

Gear Ratio Table for a Bike with 26-inch Wheels

Number of teeth in the front sprocket or chainring

Number of Teeth in the Rear Sprocket or Freewheel	24	28	32	36	39	41	43	45	47	49	51	53
13	48	56	64	72	82	86	90	94	98	102	106	
15	42	49	55	62	68	71	75	78	81	85	88	92
17	37	43	49	55	60	63	66	69	72	75	78	81
19	33	38	44	49	53	56	59	62	64	67	70	73
21	30	35	40	45	48	51	53	56	58	61	63	66
23	27	32	36	41	44	46	49	51	53	55	58	60
25	25	29	33	37	41	43	45	47	49	51	53	55
27	23	27	31	35	38	39	41	43	45	47	49	51
28	22	26	30	33	36	38	40	42	44	46	47	49
32	20	23	26	29	32	33	35	37	38	40	41	43
38	16	19	22	25	27	28	29	31	32	33	35	36

the smallest inside chainring with the smallest outside cog. Using either extreme bends the chain out of alignment. If such warping doesn't throw the chain or make disturbing noises, it certainly will cause excessive wear on both the chain and sprockets. So use gear ratios that keep the chain reasonably aligned fore and aft.

Say you are faced by a slope covered with loose dirt. Aside from trying to climb it without being tuckered out, your big job will be trying to keep solid traction on the rear wheel. It may help if you let a little air out of your knobbies, particularly the rear tire. Take it down to, say, about 25 psi, where it yields to moderate thumb pressure. Thus, semi-flattened, your tires mush into the dirt, increasing the size of the footprint and putting more of the knobs on the ground to help grip the loose dirt. Of course, soft tires make hard pedaling, and you will need to use a low gear to provide needed climbing power. You will probably want to use your small chainring and a large cog . . . your granny gears. You will have to pedal fast, but it won't require massive strength to get up the hill. Use your past experience and pick your gear ratio before you start up the slope. Once you are under way and putting heavy pressure on the pedals, shifting becomes extremely difficult and tough on derailleurs.

While ascending, you use a different climbing posture than you do on pavement, where there is firm traction. You want to stay in the saddle as long as you can. Lean forward to steer and put power in the pedals, but stay seated to keep plenty of weight back and over the rear wheel where you need it for traction. If you have lowered your saddle for an earlier descent, before starting your climb, it's a good idea to raise the saddle to a height where you are still able to get full power strokes from your legs without standing up and leaning forward—a sure way to encourage your rear wheel to spin out from under you on a steep dirt slope. This does not mean that there aren't times when standing up and peddling doesn't help you

With your weight forward, you are apt to lose traction on the rear wheel.

On dirt hills stay seated with weight over the rear wheel to maintain traction.

get up a hill. It simply depends on the hill and the riding surface beneath your tires.

Through trial-and-error, you will soon learn the climbing techniques that will provide you with ample power and speed for any type of soft or rocky terrain. You will learn to shift gears even under mild climbing conditions, although shifting is far easier when you can release the pressure on the pedals.

You will find it is best to do most of your shifting with the rear cogs, calling upon the forward chainrings for major changes in gear ratios. Above all, shift only one gear at a time. Don't try to slam through several gear changes in one fell swoop. For most steep uphill challenges you should use your granny gears. With them you will be able to climb anything the back tire will stick to.

If none of this works, you can dismount and push your bike the rest of the way. Or you can simply pick it up and carry it to the top. Pushing is pushing. But to carry, or portage, your bike, lift it up from the left side, away from the sharp-toothed chainwheel. Put your arm through the frame just beneath the saddle, resting the frame on your shoulder. Steady the handlebars or stem with your right hand, and move on. Some bikes are equipped with a shoulder carrying strap or a portage pad, which is easier on your shoulder.

There is nothing embarrassing about pushing or carrying your all-terrain bike. In fact, you will find times when it is the only way you will be able to ford a stream, cross a ravine, or get to the top of a hill that is too steep to bull your way up even in your lowest granny gears.

Actually, climbing a hill is less scary than going down it. About the worst that can happen in a climb is for you to lose traction, stall out, lose your balance, and topple over on your side. When descending, however, both gravity and momentum gang up in an attempt to send you plummeting out of control toward the bottom of the hill. The secret to a safe and sane descent is to keep firm control over your bike at all times.

Off-road biking lifts the spirit of adventure. *Gant Corporation*

In preparing for the descent, loosen the quick-release clamp on the saddle. Having raised the saddle for the earlier climb, you now lower it down out of the way and retighten the clamp. Check your brake pads and positive lever action. Without good brakes you won't stand a chance of keeping your metal steed from plunging out of control.

You might pump some air back into your tires to firm them up. Traction is not so important going downhill. You are bound to do quite a bit of skidding trying to follow a steeply descending course. But controlled skidding is part of the fun and challenge of a downhill run. Besides, if your tires are underinflated they are apt to jump the rims, which is a sure way to end your ride.

As you start down, stand on your pedals, with the cranks in horizontal position so that they are clear of the dirt, rocks, and most vegetation. This position also provides good balance and allows you to use your bent knees as shock absorbers.

Keep your chest down and your rear end back and low. If you allow your weight to go forward, you set yourself up to take a header if the front wheel hits a rut or suddenly tears the handlebars from your grip. Never apply your front brake first, and use it sparingly—just enough to maintain control over the front wheel. A hard squeeze may pitch you right over the handlebars. When approaching a rut, let off the front brake—usually controlled by

Coasting downhill is mostly a matter of leveling the pedals and maintaining good brake control.

All-terrain riders on a West African cycling safari visit a group of young natives. *David Moser*

your left brake lever—and roll over it as you pull up on the handlebars to unweight the front wheel.

Meanwhile, use your rear brake as a sailor uses a sea anchor— to slow down and stay steady on course. Unless you are deliberately bent on skidding around a turn, apply the rear brake short of starting a slide. Steer primarily by using body lean; the handlebars will follow naturally.

The steeper the descent, the farther back you want to be on the bike. Slide back off the seat and suspend yourself over the rear wheel. Thus, having lowered your center of gravity, you play the brakes carefully. Never let momentum get away from you.

These are some of the basics for all-terrain bicycling. When you have mastered them, you will have no trouble with your off-road riding, no matter how smooth or rough the terrain.

So, use your all-terrain bike for all purposes. Take day rides close to home. Haul your bike to the mountains, the desert, or the seashore. Use it in the dirt, sand, rocks, and water. Take half-day trips, weekend journeys, or long vacations on it. Your all-terrain bike will serve you well on all occasions. Use it boldly whenever and wherever you want. It will provide you with the maximum in pedal-powered fun and excitement.

7

Bike Care

Even though an all-terrain bike is one of the most rugged and durable pedal-powered machines yet made, it is susceptible to problems that any bicycle may suffer. You can avoid most problems by keeping your bike clean, properly adjusted, and in good repair. Most things you can do yourself, but some are better left to an experienced bicycle mechanic. You usually find such a person at your local bike shop.

If you make full use of your bike's capabilities for off-road riding, it is bound to get a bit messed up. But there is no excuse for letting your vehicle stay dirty, grimy, or splashed with oil. Give it a regular cleaning. Use soap and water, patience and elbow grease. A rag and a small brush to get into tight places are probably all you will need to keep it clean. Avoid using solvent or paint thinner, except when you are trying to remove oil or grease. Most petroleum by-products are hard on paint finishes. If they get into the bearings, they quickly dilute or flush out the essential lubricating grease. Never hose off your bike. Clean it by hand. Although many of the components may be rustproof alloys, some may not be. So make it a practice to wipe your bike dry after cleaning it.

One very important chore is to keep your tires properly inflated and in good shape. Today's fat tires are well built and usually take almost as much pressure as skinny racing tires. For pavement

Sometimes you may have to rely on an experienced bicycle mechanic.

riding you can inflate some fat tires all the way up to 50 or 60 psi of pressure. Some ATB tires are made that will withstand up to 80 psi. Much depends upon the size and quality of the tire; so check with your bike shop.

Always beware of letting too much air out of a tire, or it may slip off the rim, pinch the inner tube, or tear out the *valve stem.* Generally speaking, you should abide by the recommended pressure usually embossed or printed on the sidewall of the tire. On hot days, riding over scorching pavement, it's wise to lower the pressure about 5 pounds to allow for heat expansion.

Even balloon tires don't take much air. Be very careful when filling them that you don't overinflate. A good high-pressure hand pump with a built-in gauge does a good job of controlling inflation. But such pumps are usually too big to haul around with you. On the road or trail you should carry a regular lightweight bicycle pump that clamps on the frame, out of the way. You can carry a small gauge in your tool kit. However, even without a gauge you soon learn to use the thumb-and-finger pinch method to tell pretty well when your tire is decently inflated. In the field, where any inflation is better than none, you don't have to be too critical.

Try to avoid using gas station air hoses. High-pressure service station pumps often will pop your tire before you know what's happened. By the time you are able to make out the gauge reading, it may be too late. However, if no other air source is available, just be careful to put the air into your tire in short spurts, testing after each spurt to determine the tire's firmness.

Although off-road tires are larger and more durable than the frail skinny tires of ten-speed lightweights, you can count on having a certain number of punctures. And you will find that most of

Pay attention to proper tire inflation.

them happen at the most inconvenient times and in remote places. But if you have your patching kit and a couple of tire irons, your worst penalty will probably be a slight delay.

When you can find the puncture quickly, you needn't remove the tire completely in order to fix it. Lay the bike on its side, or stand it upside down. Let all of the air out of the tire. Turn the wheel so the puncture is handy to reach. Marking the spot, you can safely remove the sharp object.

Pry the bead away from one side of the rim so you can reach and pull out at least enough tube to expose the puncture hole. Rough up the area around the hole. Apply a thin coat of the rubber cement that comes with the kit. Let it dry for several minutes. Then peel the protective backing off the adhesive side of a patch and press the patch firmly in place over the puncture. Check the inside of the casing for any foreign matter. Reinsert the tube and, being careful not to pinch the tube between the bead and the rim, work the tire back into the wheel.

Slow leaks are sometimes difficult to locate. Occasionally you may need to remove the inner tube, pump a little air into it, and find some water to dunk it in. You can easily find the leak by tracing the rising bubbles to their source. Sometimes you can dampen a suspected leak with saliva and watch for telltale bubbles. Just be sure that if you remove a wheel, particularly the back wheel, that you are careful not to separate the parts any more than is necessary; they must all be reassembled in exact reverse sequence.

Once you've located the slow leak—by bubble or faint hiss—do the normal patching job. Leaving just enough air in the tube to give it shape, reinsert it carefully in the tire. Start with the valve stem and pry the tire beads back into place, then inflate it.

Since tire problems are certain and unpredictable, you may find it wise to carry a spare inner tube in your kit, particularly if you spend much time in the backcountry. An extra rolled-up tire takes up little room in a pack and can save you from becoming stranded.

Patching leaks and punctures is a familiar chore for any cyclist.

You also guarantee more pleasant riding if you take good care of your bike chain. It is the key element of the drivetrain mechanism. A bicycle chain is made up of rollers, plates, bushings, and rivets. The average chain has approximately 500 separate pieces—about as many parts as there are in a Rolls-Royce engine. You wouldn't let your Rolls get all stuck up with dirt, grit, sand, and grime, so don't let your bicycle chain.

A dirty, poorly adjusted chain can rob up to 10 percent of the muscle energy that should be going into powering your bike. Sand and grime will not only wear out a chain quickly, but they will also grind away at the teeth of your chainrings and rear cogs. So keep your chain clean and lubricated. You will save a lot of trouble and expense.

The simplest way to do this is to use solvent or paint thinner and a toothbrush on the chain while it is still on the bike. By going carefully at it, top and bottom, you can free most of the dirt from the chain mechanism. Use plenty of old newspaper underneath to catch the drips. Take particular pains getting to the chain's moving parts—the rollers, bushings, and rivets. Wipe the chain clean, and go over it again.

While you're cleaning the chain, do the best you can with solvent and brush to tidy up the chainrings, cogs, and derailleurs, all of which collect oily grime.

When you are satisfied that everything is as clean as you can get it, and you have dried it thoroughly, it's time to lubricate. Use a light oil that will penetrate the pins and rollers. Use it sparingly. Heavily lubricated chains merely collect more dust and dirt. You can use a

A little chain lubrication helps provide a smooth, trouble-free ride.

special spray-on bicycle lubricant. Daubing on a little light mineral oil also works fine. A short spurt or a single drop, link by link, does the job.

If you want to go to the trouble, you can melt some ordinary paraffin used in canning fruits and vegetables. While still hot, brush it onto your chain so that it penetrates deeply into the joints. The wax not only lubricates, but collects less grime.

This is a good time to adjust your chain so it has about a half-inch of up-and-down play when you lift the top center links with your finger. With correct tension, the chain won't squeak, clatter, jump a sprocket, or bind. You can usually adjust chain tension with the rear derailleur. But derailleurs differ greatly, so study the instructions in your owner's manual before you attack with a screwdriver.

The second and more thorough method for cleaning and lubricating a chain requires that you remove it from your bike. Then you can soak or douse it thoroughly in a pan of paint thinner or cleaning solvent. Kerosene is all right, but it has a tendency to leave a dust-gathering film on the chain. *Never use gasoline to clean any parts of your bike!* It is extremely flammable and dangerous. In fact, even when using any of the thinners or solvents, do so outdoors where there is ample ventilation, and keep well away from any source of fire.

To remove the thin chain on a derailleur-equipped bike, you need to separate a link. It is sometimes more convenient to take off the rear wheel so you can remove the chain. Modern narrow bike chains seldom have a master link. This means you must use a special small and inexpensive chain tool to push out one of the rivets, or push it far enough out to separate the link. Don't shove it all the way through or you will have a heck of a time putting the chain back together. If you are inexperienced in working with chains, you had better get a little help.

With the chain removed from the bike, bathe it well in whatever oil and grime dissolvent you prefer, hang it out to dry, then get to the lubing. If you like the paraffin method, you can dip the whole chain in and hang it up to drip-dry while the paraffin is still hot so the excess wax runs off. While the chain is off the bike, you can do a really good job of spiffing up the sprockets, derailleurs, and any other exposed parts.

When you reinstall the rear wheel, line it up so the chain is in a straight line with the front and back of your bike. To do this, loop the chain around the midfront and midrear sprockets. This should put the chain in proper alignment so it can be shifted up or down without bending it excessively or causing the chain to jump sprockets.

If, however, the chain is inclined to shift too far either way and starts slipping off the cogs, you can usually correct it by carefully tuning either of the two adjusting screws located in easy reach on the derailleur. Usually the top screw adjusts for the small cog or high gear, while the bottom screw adjusts for the low gear or biggest cog. There are similar screws on the front derailleur to keep the chain from jumping beyond the small or large chainrings. Adjusting a derailleur is a delicate but not difficult operation—particularly if you follow the instructions in your owner's manual. But, beyond simple adjustments, leave derailleur problems to an experienced bicycle mechanic. A fouled, bent, or chronically ill-adjusted derailleur becomes a source of constant anguish to any bicyclist.

Occasionally wheel spokes will loosen. If not corrected, a few loose spokes can twist a wheel out of line. And, once a wheel is warped, it takes an expert to remove the wobble and get it rolling straight again. To prevent this, occasionally sound out your spokes to determine if any have started to loosen up. Spin the wheel and drag a screwdriver or your fingernail lightly over the spokes. They should *ping* in pretty much the same key. If one *pongs*, tighten it up a bit with your spoke wrench. You can sometimes correct a slight off-balance bulge in the rim by tightening a couple of spokes on the opposite side. But do it gradually. Major wheel realignments should be left to a skilled wheelman.

Other simple maintenance jobs involve keeping all of the nuts, bolts, and screws properly tightened to eliminate squeaks, grinds, rattles, and wear. Check the assorted brake and gearshift cables. Use a drop of lubricant at the various points where they disappear into or emerge out of an outer casing. Keep the thumb shifters clean and lubricated also. Use your Allen wrenches to tighten the bolts on your handlebar stem, chainrings, brake cables, or anything else secured by the sunken-headed screws.

Check your brakes. Take up a little on the cables if there is excessive play, or if you have to squeeze the brake levers all the way to the handlebar grips before the brakes take a firm hold. Replace worn *brake shoes* as needed. They are inexpensive and easy to carry in your tool kit. It's foolish to skimp on brake pads, because

Off-road cyclists take pride in their bikes.

A clean, well-tuned bike is a joy to ride.

being unable to stop quickly may wreck your bike, to say nothing of causing you injury. Also, keep your wheel rims clean so that your brake shoes will get a firm grip.

If your saddle is leather, try to keep it from getting wet and treat it with a waterproofing formula to preserve the leather. If the saddle is covered with polyethylene or soft vinyl, you need not worry because water won't hurt it. Keep your saddle clean and properly adjusted.

There are many things you can and should do to keep your all-terrain bike looking good and in top running order. But, unless you have an exceptional mechanical aptitude, there probably are things you should think twice about before tackling. For instance, sealed bearings are great things to have to keep the mud, slush, sand, and water out of wheel hubs, the bottom bracket, the headset, and sometimes the pedals. But even sealed bearings can become gummed up. They are packed in grease, not oil. Servicing them properly usually is a job for a mechanic. However, when not tampered with, sealed bearings last a long time and need not be a major concern.

All in all, though it may sound a bit complicated, taking care of your all-terrain bike is not difficult. Do things that you can do comfortably and sensibly and that are not apt to put your bike too far out of whack if you slip up slightly. You will be gaining experience, and in time you will become an expert in your own right.

8

Observed Trials

t is barely dawn when two of your cyclist friends stop by to pick you up. You strap your all-terrain bike next to the two already racked securely atop the four-door sports sedan that will transport you out to the hills where that day's off-road competitions are scheduled to take place. You hop in and start out.

An hour later, the morning sun is just beginning to nibble the dew from the beaded grass when you turn off the highway and onto a dirt road. After jostling along for a half-mile, you reach the rocky parking area where a growing group of cyclists are busily unloading their all-terrain bikes and getting them ready for the day's events. Both young men and women keep up a steady flow of cheerful banter as they work.

As soon as the bikes are tightened and tuned, their owners ride over to the sign-up shelter to register and pay a small entry fee for whatever event or events they have chosen to participate in. Competition has been scheduled to take place throughout the day. There will be an assortment of beginners, experts, and pros of all sizes and ages: men, women, boys, and girls.

The meet is officially sanctioned by NORBA. NORBA formulates off-road policies; establishes safety requirements; helps lay out the obstacle courses; sanctions and promotes various state, regional, and national championships. With nominal membership dues NORBA provides active legislative representation on behalf of both competitive and recreational off-road bicyclists, in addition to its other benefits.

Prominently displayed at the sign-up tent is a boldly printed sign directing all bikers to wear a hard-shell helmet. The contestants are dressed in a colorful array of bicycling clothing and shoes. Most have protective gloves tucked temporarily into pockets. Since the day is expected to turn quite warm, many wear mid-thigh-length biking shorts and short-sleeved jerseys. A few wear long-sleeved shirts and long pants, seeming to prefer the heat to the risk of sunburn or scratches from the trees and spiny bushes covering much of the two separate courses that have been laid out days earlier.

One is a short *observed trials* course. It is made up of several segments, or *sections*, of assorted obstacles, including boulders,

Signing up before the competition.

logs, water, mud, or whatever else a fiendish course designer was able to dream up. The second course is a winding, uphill, downhill, and hazard-cluttered trail laid out to test the skills and endurance of the long-distance racers.

One of your friends signs up for the observed trials. Unlike the racing competition, the trials pit the cyclist against the short but difficult course. Running trials is a test of slow-speed bike control and precise riding skill. The "observed" part merely means that the rider is watched, judged, and scored by official checkers.

"Boy, it's going to be a tough run," your friend says on his return from having walked around the trials course to check it out. Although he is allowed to walk it, he is not permitted to ride over the course ahead of time. "It's loaded with rocks, roots, sand, logs, hills, drop-offs, and . . . well, you name it. It's more for motorcycles than bikes."

That could be. Maybe motorcycles have used it before. The trials event was borrowed from dirt-bike motorcyclists who have been riding such obstacle courses for years. The concept is simple: You need only make your way over, around, or through assorted blockades, hazards, and hurdles without dabbing a foot to the ground, tumbling over, or coming to a stop—all of which either costs penalty points or results in disqualification.

Spectators enjoy the trials because most of the action takes place within easy viewing.

As your friend checks out his bike while awaiting his turn, you climb a knoll from which you see most of the trials course. You watch as, one at a time, the first three bikers tackle the nearest section of the course. The first rider does well, jumping over rocks, climbing a stump, and splashing through a hub-deep creek while staying within bounds of the ribboned-off sections. You can tell that he knows what he's doing.

Although speed is not of the essence, the second rider takes too slow and deliberate a pace. Twice when confronted by a tangle of

A trials rider dabs a foot for a penalty point. *Charles R. Kelly*

gnarled roots across the trail, he lets his momentum falter and dabs a foot to the ground to maintain his balance. With each dab the official section observer puts pencil to clipboard, and you know he's jotting penalty points on his scoresheet. You also know that the rider who finishes with the fewest points wins.

On the sharp hairpin curve at the bottom of a steep downhill slope, the third rider tries to make a jump turn by hopping his bike off the ground and swinging it around in midair. But he loses control, swerves off the marked course and out of the event.

Now it's your friend's turn. Seeming to have studied what has gone on before, he adjusts his speed in order to enter the first

Not everyone makes it through a trials course. *Charles R. Kelly*

Trials riding puts both bike and rider to some strenuous tests. *Charles R. Kelly*

Up and over a log barrier. *Fat Tire Flyer/Charles R. Kelly*

section with just the right momentum to hoist himself over a large boulder blocking the course. The bash-plate that protects the chainrings from being crunched scrapes heavily against the top of the rock, then skids off the far side. Seeming elated at not having to dab to get over the rock, your buddy makes a successful pogolike spin-turn at the bottom, and heads for the creek.

He again accelerates, obviously hoping to get through the hub-deep water before it drags him down. As he hits the stream, disappearing into the spray, the front tire apparently slips on a mossy stone. To regain his balance, he has to dab a foot briefly into the stream, but not quickly enough to prevent the observer from marking down a penalty point.

From there on, for as long as you are able to keep him in view, you watch your friend tackle a series of barriers in other sections of the trials course. He approaches a jumbled stack of short pieces of logs laid across the narrow trail. Just before his front tire reaches the first segment, he heaves up on the handlebars and goes into a steep wheelie. As the front wheel tops the first log, he suddenly thrusts himself up off the saddle and heaves forward while pushing down on the handlebars. This unweights the whole aft section of the bike and brings the rear wheel up onto the log. With another rocking motion, he horses the bike up onto the second of the stepped-up logs. Then, just before he loses momentum, he bounces cleanly down the far side of the barrier. A clean jump! He pedals on across a short neutral zone separating one trials course section from another. He pedals slowly, obviously trying to catch his breath before tackling the next series of obstacles.

Although you doubt that he can hear it through the shouts and cheers of the spectators, you call encouragement. Wishing your friend success, you mount your bike and pedal toward the racing course where a large group of riders are gathering. The trials are exciting to watch, but you have your own race to run. And you know that it will be a tough one.

9

Mud, Sweat, and Gears

Rules of racing competition allow you to take a trial run on the course to familiarize yourself with its challenges and obstacles. You put your bike into a low gear and take your time pedaling over the route. You carefully study the layout of ruts and ravines, steep slopes, and sheer drop-offs. You try to mark each tree, bush, and rock in your memory; it will all help later on.

The course is a 2-mile circuit that winds uphill, downhill, and crosshill. It gains and loses nearly 500 feet each lap, which means a lot of climbing and downslope running. For a while the course follows a narrow cattle trail that cuts along a dirt ledge, then drops off suddenly into a ravine. It follows along the zigzagging bottom of the ravine until it reaches the creek downstream from where the observed trials riders have been making their crossings. From the creek the trail crosses a flat stretch marked by a windmill and a cattle-watering tank. Then quite abruptly it rises up a long steep hill. You doubt that many will be able to pedal all the way to the top.

You continue on around the course. Slowly. Saving your strength for the real race ahead.

During the next couple of hours a series of preliminary races are run to sift out the finalists for later on. Sports-class riders, made up mostly of those who just want to get out and challenge the terrain, tear around the course in a four-lap event. There is a veterans' race for those between the ages of thirty-five and forty-four. There is even a masters' race for people older than that. Pros and amateurs often compete against each other in pro-am events. Men and women usually race separately, but not always. Both men and women enter some races, and there are plenty of women who give the men a real run for it.

But, as the day lengthens, you are less concerned with the many categories than you are with getting ready for the finals. Having come in third in a preliminary heat, you are entered in the big one. While waiting for the call, you check your bike over carefully. You look over the brakes and feel the firm cable tension through the handlebar levers. You tighten down a bit on the thumb-shifter ratchets so they won't involuntarily slip and change gears during

An off-road race course is fraught with challenges. *Charles R. Kelly*

Off-road racers gather for the start. *Gant Corporation*

what is certain to be a rough ride. You check chain tension, a half-inch play up and down—no more, no less. You determine that nothing is loose or overly tight on your bike.

Suddenly the call comes over the public address system, "Last call for finalists in the pro-am. All entrants please report to the starting line."

Satisfied that your bike is ready, you mount up and ride over to the Start/Finish line, a white ribbon of powdered lime crossing the trail beneath a broad banner strung between two tall posts.

Nearly forty entrants have gathered around the spot. It's a sizeable group for any race. The real pros are placed up front. It's a privileged position. They won't have to fight their way up through the slower riders, such as yourself. The rest of the racers, including you, line up behind the pros.

Starters jockey for position.

"Get set!" the starter calls.

Quickly, you tighten the chin strap of your helmet, tug your gloves on tight, and set the right pedal at a two-o'clock position for a leg-thrusting getaway. You note that a few bikers are using drop handlebars like those seen on racing or touring ten-speeds. Several even have toe clips on their pedals, a bit risky, it seems, if they have to free their feet suddenly from the pedals. You prefer riding in a more upright position so you can see the hazards that lie ahead. And you stick with your open rattrap pedals.

Bang!

The starter's gun sets the field in frantic motion. Amid grunts, shouts, and the clank of metal, the pedalers surge forward in unison. You find yourself jockeying for position in the middle of the pack, striving for maneuvering room. Fifty yards down the slope a string of barriers funnels the cyclists into a zigzag chicane. Still closely bunched, the sudden jamming on of brakes as the bikes go into the turn triggers a chain of collisions. You swerve out wide just in time to escape the clash of metal and flying bodies. You don't glance back, but from the horrendous sounds you guess that perhaps ten bikers have bitten the dust. You also know that most won't stay down. If their machines are still intact, they will be up and rolling before the dust settles. You use the moments to find riding room and settle into your pace as the field starts to string out.

At the bottom of the first slope, the course makes a sharp switchback to the left. You hit gravel. As your bike starts to skid out from under you, you steer a hard right to regain control. You swing out onto a level stretch of an old cattle trail. Shifting to a high gear, you pump for all you're worth. You overtake and pass three riders. A little farther on you pass a rider who has thrown his chain and pulled off the trail. He struggles to disentangle the chain and get back into the race. Rules do not allow him to accept outside help.

You come suddenly upon a steep drop-off. You approach it blindly, but, having been there before, you know what to expect. What you don't know, though, is that there's a bike piled up at the bottom of the drop-off. As soon as you're close enough to peer over the rim, you see him and shout "Coming through!"

The startled downed rider looks up, sees your front wheel dropping off the ledge, and jerks his bike off the trail just in time. You level your pedals so they won't dig into the embankment. You stand up on them, putting equal weight on each. As you thrust your body far back off the seat and push down on the handlebars, the bike drops out from beneath you. Plunging almost straight down, you squeeze your rear brake lever, while using your front brake sparingly so it will not lock up and propel you over the handlebars in a header. At the bottom of the steep decline, you release brakes, maintain momentum, and pedal hard up the far side.

Suddenly you top out onto a mesa. You see a dozen or so other

A temporarily stalled racer works over a thrown chain.

cyclists strung out on the almost level trail ahead. You shift to a small rear cog to increase your gear ratio, and take out after them. Along a relatively smooth part of the trail, you reach down onto the frame, pluck one of the plastic water bottles from its cage, and quickly squirt a drink into your dry mouth. Replacing the bottle, you bend back to your task.

Suddenly, while going full tilt, you charge into a sharp right-hand turn before you have time to prepare. Going excessively fast, you lock your brakes, lean low, and throw your machine into an end-switching skid. Trying to keep from careening off the course and piling into a clump of spiny bushes, you dab your inside foot to keep from tumbling. As you regain balance, shift up a notch, and continue on your way, the cheers of trailside spectators ring in your ears.

With weight well back, a racer descends a short but steep drop-off.

After a quick fix of his flat, the rider will get back in the race.

Beyond the next rise you come upon the other friend who had picked you up early that morning. He is frantically working on a flat tire. You're sorry, but you can't stop and help. You shout encouragement to him and pedal on past.

By now your legs are bundles of aching muscles. Your lungs burn. Sweat pours down your face and back. As you thread your way through a stretch of scratchy underbrush, you are thankful for your helmet, ankle-length riding pants, and long-sleeved jersey.

Then you come to a welcome breather, a stretch of gentle downhill slope that, although corduroyed and rough, you take easily by standing on your leveled pedals and letting your bike buck mildly and absorb the shock beneath you.

You approach a line of willows marking the creek. Before reaching the water, you have already decided that it is shallow enough to attempt riding through, rather than having to dismount and walk your bike through. Quickly you shift down to a low gear and increase pedal rotation. The lower gear should prevent you from stalling out halfway across.

Despite the low gear, you hit the creek at a fast enough pace to send sheets of water flying to both sides of your wheels. Much of it comes back down on you with invigorating coolness.

Reaching the far bank, the course winds through a field of weeds and old stubble, then swings right past the creaking windmill and old cattle-watering tank. No cattle are in sight, but a rider is sitting on the ground with his back leaning against the cool moist tank. As far as you can see there doesn't seem to be anything wrong with his bike.

"I'm pooped," he says, apparently reading the wonder in your eyes. "I've had it. Legs cramped up. No way I could make that hill." He points to the long slope rising steeply up ahead. "No way!"

In truth, he looks out of shape. Off-road racing makes big demands on both your mind and body. If you're a little slack in preparing, you're apt not to hack it. And this is just the first lap of a five-lap, ten-mile race.

Without comment, you flip your quick-release and raise your saddle to provide your legs maximum leverage for the climb ahead. As the trail steepens, you shift down to your lowest granny gear.

A rushing creek does not stop an off-road racer. *Cannondale Corporation*

If the hill is too steep to pedal up, push or carry your bike.

You keep most of your weight back on the saddle, churn your pedals fast, and move slowly forward and up. With your weight back, the rear wheel holds its traction. As the slope steepens still more, you gasp and grunt and bear down harder on the pedals. You labor past a racer who has dismounted and is pushing her bike.

"Good luck," she gasps. "It's a wall up ahead."

A dozen or so yards farther on, you pedal past another walker, only this one is carrying his bike slung over his shoulder.

"You must have had your Wheaties this morning," he shouts, as you puff your way past. "Hang in there, pal."

But you cannot hang in very long. A few yards farther on, you simply cannot sit back in the saddle and keep the pedals rotating. So you rise up, lean forward, and put more weight on the pedals. You

On a level stretch of mesa, racers go all out for the finish line.

are able to keep on for about fifty feet when—zip—the back wheel loses traction and starts spinning beneath you. The bike stalls, stops, and starts to topple over. You vault off it and start pushing. This is one whale of a hill!

But, without giving it much thought, you realize that the first lap is nearly finished. You know, too, that you have already passed about a dozen of the contestants strung out along the course behind you. This boosts your hopes.

You reach the top of the hill and pause to take a few deep breaths. Then you remount and accelerate along the trail leading toward the distant banners that mark the Start/Finish line.

Shifting once more to a high gear, you snake your way through a thicket of chaparral, break out into the open, and go all out toward the line.

You're dead-tired. You ache from your ears to your feet. Your mouth is cotton-dry and you're sweat-soaked. It has turned hot. Trickles of sweat soak your face and body. But, for all that, you feel good. And you're not worried about the next four laps. As soon as you get your second wind, you should be able to handle the future demands of the race.

As you streak under the banner, concluding the first lap, you are spurred on by the cheers of the spectators. You smile to yourself. You really feel alive. You know now exactly why you got up before dawn to come out into the hills to pit your strength and riding skills against others who share the same interest and competitive drive. It's a real challenge, and it's a lot of fun and excitement. And that's what off-road biking is all about.

You thrust your feet hard onto the pedals and surge ahead. There is still a race to be won.

Glossary

Allen wrench—a six-sided, usually L-shaped key made to fit Allen-headed screws.

All-terrain—any and all types of land surface.

ATB—an all-terrain bicycle built especially for rough-country riding; also an off-road, fat-tire, or mountain bike.

Boss—the brazed-on fittings for attaching brakes and other accessories to a bike frame.

Bottom bracket—a short tube at the lowest part of the frame that holds the crankset.

Brake lever—a hand-operated lever mounted on the handlebars to actuate the brake.

Brake pad—the rubber block that presses against the rim for braking action.

Brake shoe—the metal portion of the brake that holds the brake pads in place.

Braze-ons—the small nubs brazed to the frame for attaching assorted items.

Butted—tubing or spokes that are thicker at one end than in the middle.

Cables—the control wires leading to brakes or derailleurs.

Cantilever brake—a reliable rim-squeezing friction brake.

Center of gravity—the central balancing point of an object.

Centerpull brake—a brake controlled evenly by a single central cable.

Chain—the connected links that transmit power through the sprockets to the rear wheel.

Chainrings—individual sprockets that make up the chainwheel.

Chain stays—rear frame members reaching from the bottom bracket to the back wheel dropouts.

Chainwheel—the large front sprocket assembly, often made up of two or three chainrings.

Clincher—a wire-beaded tire-and-tube combination.

Clunker—an affectionate term given to early all-terrain bikes.

Cluster—the nest of small sprocket cogs in the freewheel assembly.

Cog—a rear-wheel sprocket element.

Components—the assorted parts that make up a bicycle.

Crank—the foot-rotated bar to which pedals are attached.

Crankset—the bottom bracket assembly made up of cranks, chainrings, spindle, and bearings.

Dab—to lower a foot to the ground or to use other support during trials competition.

Derailleur—a mechanism that moves or "derails" the chain from one sprocket to another.

Double-butted—tubing that is thicker at both ends.

Down tube—the forward part of the frame reaching from the head tube to the bottom bracket.

Drivetrain—the power-producing assembly composed of pedals, sprockets, chain, and the rear wheel.

Dropouts—the wheel axle slots located at the end of the front forks and the rear chain stays.

Endo—a trick maneuver in which the cyclist locks the front brake, unweights the rear wheel, and balances up on the front wheel only.

English racer—early term for lightweight gearshift bicycle.

Fat tire—slang for balloon tire.

Fat-tire bike—see *ATB*.

Fork—the two-pronged tube that holds the front wheel and is turned by the handlebars.

Freewheel—the clutchlike sprocket mounted on the rear wheel hub.

Gear ratio—the amount of movement produced by combining assorted sizes of front and rear sprockets.

Gonzo—slang for carefree, all-out all-terrain biking.

Gooseneck—the part that fits into the head tube and holds the handlebars.

Granny gears—the combination of a small chainring plus a large rear cog that produces a powerful but slow gear ratio.

Handlebar stem—see *Gooseneck*.

Headset—consists of adjusting nuts, cones, and the front fork bearings in which the handlebars turn.

Head tube—the short forward member of the main frame that connects the top tube and the down tube; it contains front forks and headset parts.

Hub—the front or rear wheel centers, drilled to hold the spokes and contain the axle bearings.

Inner tube—a rubber or Butyl airtight tube used inside a clincher tire.

Kickstand—a foldout support for holding a bicycle upright.

Knobbies—tires with heavy lugged treads; good for dirt riding.

Lug—reinforcing sleeves at the frame tubing joints.

Mountain bike—see *ATB*.

Observed trials—monitored low-speed competition over an obstacle course.

Off-road bike—see *ATB*.

Quick-release—a mechanism for fast removal or change of wheels or saddle.

Rattrap pedals—tooth-edged, basic, no-frills cage pedals.

Rear triangle—the part of the frame formed by the seat tube, the chain stays, and the seat stays.

Rim—the basic wheel minus the spokes, hub, or tires.

Roller-cam brake—a reliable, strong, centerpull-type brake.

Rolling resistance—the tendency of a tire to cling to the riding surface.

Saddle—a bicycle seat.

Sanctioned—an event run under an association's rules.

Seat post—an adjustable seat-holding cylinder that fits into the seat tube.

Seat stays—the rear frame members extending from just under the seat to the rear wheel dropouts.

Seat tube—the part of the frame extending from under the seat to the bottom bracket.

Section—a short segment of an observed trials course.

Sprocket—a toothed wheel turned by the chain.

Stem—see *Gooseneck*.

Stunting—doing bicycle tricks such as wheelies, endos, et cetera.

Thumb shifter—the gearshift levers mounted on the handlebars.

Tire irons—the leverlike tools used to pry the tire off the rim.

Toe clips—a cage on the pedals; not normally used in all-terrain biking.

Top tube—the horizontal main frame tube reaching from the seat tube to the head tube.

Traction—the ability of a tire to grip the riding surface.

Valve stem—an inner-tube attachment through which air is pumped.

Velocipede—an archaic name for a two-wheeled, pedal-powered vehicle.

Wheelbase—the distance between the front and rear wheel centers.

Wheelie—a trick maneuver in which the cyclist lifts the front wheel and rides on the rear wheel only.

Information Sources

National Off-Road Bicycle Association (NORBA)
Box 1901
Chandler, AZ 85244

Fat-Tire Flyer Magazine
P.O. Box 757
Fairfax, CA 94930

Bicycling Magazine
33 E. Minor Street
Emmaus, PA 18049

Bicycle Rider Magazine
29901 Agoura Road
Agoura, CA 91301

Cyclist Magazine
20916 Higgins Court
Torrance, CA 90501

Index

Page numbers in *italics* refer to illustrations.